CW01511412

REAL-LIFE
SCENIC TECHNIQUES
FOR
MODEL RAILROADERS

REAL-LIFE
SCENIC TECHNIQUES
FOR
MODEL RAILROADERS

CARL CAIATI

TAB BOOKS Inc.
Blue Ridge Summit, PA

To my dearest wife Julie, who I love and enjoy even more than model railroading.

and

To Nora, the greatest kid sister anyone could ever have.

FIRST EDITION
SECOND PRINTING

Copyright © 1987 by TAB BOOKS Inc.
Printed in the United States of America

Reproduction or publication of the content in any manner, without express
permission of the publisher, is prohibited. No liability is assumed with respect to
the use of the information herein.

Library of Congress Cataloging in Publication Data

Caiati, Carl.
Real-life scenic techniques for model railroaders.

Bibliography: p.
Includes index.
1. Railroads—Models. I. Title.
TF197.C27 1986   625.1'9   86-6000
ISBN 0-8306-2765-0 (pbk.)

TAB BOOKS Inc. offers software for
sale. For information and a catalog,
please contact TAB Software Department,
Blue Ridge Summit, PA 17294-0850.

Questions regarding the content of this book
should be addressed to:

Reader Inquiry Branch
TAB BOOKS Inc.
Blue Ridge Summit, PA 17294-0214

Contents

Foreword

Model railroading has always been a fascinating hobby, a hobby which has few if any equals for total absorption from the cares of business and the screaming headlines which bombard us daily. What is it about model railroading as a hobby that makes it so fascinating?

Models of real locomotives and cars have been with us almost as long as there have been real railroads. In fact, the very first steam locomotive in America was built and operated by John Stevens in Hoboken, New Jersey on a loop of track not unlike that packed to this day with train sets. Many real locomotives began life in miniature form to prove their practicality.

As the real railroads began to move inland and on towards far-off cities, they became dream machines for young men who saw in the iron horse the means by which they could travel to distant places to achieve fame and fortune. It wasn't long before toy manufacturers realized that children of all ages were a tremendous market for toy trains. The very earliest were pull or push toys of wood and lithographed cardboard gaily colored. These

gave way to tin and cast iron models made to be pushed along the floor without track. With the invention of toy track, it became feasible to power locomotives with clockwork mechanisms and simple live steam boilers, although some powered toys were made before track was common.

By 1883 the Novelty Electric Company of Philadelphia put into production the very first commercially available train sets powered by electricity. Power was provided by a wet cell. An HO passenger car commemorating this important milestone in model railroading was produced 100 years later by *Railroad Model Craftsman* magazine to honor the event.

The first HO trains were made in Europe by Bing in 1922 and were essentially toy trains. While some magnificent scale models had been made by craftsmen skilled in metal working, it wasn't until the 1920 era that crude kits became commercially available which made scale model railroading available to a wider market. The Chicago Century of Progress of 1933 introduced scale models to millions. Suppliers such as Walthers, Mantua, George

Stock, Alexander and others soon offered kits which were capable of assembly by most home craftsmen. The year 1933 also saw the first issue *Railroad Model Craftsman* on the newsstands, and it had a tremendous influence on the growth of the hobby. *Model Railroader* was born in 1934, only one year later.

The late 1930s saw model railroading take a giant leap forward when several lines of low cost HO locomotives and cars became available using very simple construction techniques. By the early postwar years, HO had surged forward to become the most popular hobby scale.

Curiously, the growing popularity of scale model railroading saw a parallel rise in popularity of toy trains as another facet of hobby railroading. There were a large number of operators for whom building was not as much fun as operation. For them, the durability and rugged construction of Lionel and Gilbert trains were more important than the realistic appearance of scale model trains. Indeed, toy trains could be transformed into model railroads having almost as much realism as the scale equipment while retaining the advantages of sharper curves and simpler wiring inherent in toy trains.

As scale model railroading developed, cars and locomotive kits adopted many of the mass market techniques of their toy counterparts. At the same time scale modelers, feeling the need for finer detail, began developing lost wax castings and achieved previously unheard of detail. Importers discovered in Japan and later in Korea craftsmen who could turn out brass locomotives in limited quantities for modelers who wanted specialized locomotives for specific railroads. These locomotives made it possible for fans of regional railroads to acquire rosters of locomotives never before available.

An attempt was made to make trains smaller than HO after World War II, but TT gauge was only slightly smaller than HO and never achieved the popularity needed to become commercially viable. Then came N gauge, which today offers a tremendous variety of equipment. The most popular home scales continue to be HO, O, and N. Another tiny scale called Z is also available, and S gauge continues to appeal to a select group of modelers. There are also modelers in various narrow gauges, modelers who prefer trolleys, the live steam fans, and modelers who do nothing but collect train equipment.

As the builder develops his railroad in whatever scale and gauge most appeals to him, he soon realizes that he can make improvements to locomotives and cars to make them look better and more detailed, or to make them look more like the favorite locomotives he wants to model.

There are thousands of special parts available to the modeler to make customizing of cars and locomotives easy. Similar materials make scenery making and track laying and wiring easier as well. Perhaps the word easier is not entirely correct, but there are techniques that permit the modeler to do things with his own scale model railroad, or with his hobby model railroad if he prefers to work with toy trains, which the average train set owner would consider impossible. Local hobby shops carry most of these items.

Carl Caiati started his model railroading hobby almost a quarter century ago, and within a few years had developed his techniques to a point where they were seen regularly in *Railroad Model Craftsman*. Carl doesn't go overboard with tough techniques. Using commercially available equipment and components, he creates customized equipment that can't be bought. The techniques that are explained clearly and in a step-by-step manner by Carl in this book will help you to achieve the same results. Hop aboard and become another of the thousands of modelers of all ages who have discovered the wonderful world of hobby model railroading.

Harold H. Carstens
Newton, New Jersey
November 10, 1982

Acknowledgments

First and foremost I wish to thank Hal Carstens, editor and publisher of *Railroad Model Craftsman.* Our relationship goes back over 20 years to when Hal first took over the magazine, started Carstens Publications, and was instrumental in turning R.M.C. into the excellent, second-to-none model railroading periodical that it is today. Hal was also instrumental in starting me off as a writer utilizing and polishing my then "green" talents by allowing me to be an early and frequent contributor. Had I not run into Hal, this book might never have evolved.

The firm of William K. Walthers assisted greatly and without reservations through Dick Allen, who furnished necessary parts and products and allowed reproduction of some of the fine material included in the expansive Walthers catalog.

Leo Campbell of Campbell Scale Model was unstinting in his cooperation, also providing me with necessary kits from their superb line as well as fine photographs of some of their structures, which are reproduced in this book.

Without the cooperation of Howard Goodwin, president of the Lauderdale Shore Line Model R.R. Club, and the club members who are about the finest modelers around, I would not have been able to include the club material that is the "icing on the cake" of this manual. In particular, I wish to thank Howard's fellow members Doug Cline and Paul Voelker; their fine craftsmanship is also presented within these pages.

A vote of gratitude to Universal Hobbies of Fort Lauderdale, Florida, particularly Lou Kozla and Hal Jern, who were instrumental in providing necessary parts, accessories, and tools from their extensive inventory. What they did not have in stock they procured in record time with the same super service and dedication they accord their customers.

Diamond Scale Models, manufacturers of the finest turntables available, graciously assisted and provided much information and material, for which I am gratefully appreciative.

Last but by no means least, profound thanks to Cal-Scale and president John Anderson; where would a super detailing buff like me be without Cal-Scale parts and fittings?

I take off my hat to all these fine people who helped make this book possible.

Introduction

Scenery and scenic effects are to a model railroad what petals are to a flower. Granted, you can minimize or remove the petals and still have the base or the heart of the flower, but its appearance will be stark, diminished in effect, and devoid of essence. The same concept prevails in true model railroading where one wishes to approach and emulate exacting realism. Take away scenic backdrops, mountains, tunnels, terrain, trees, foliage, and water, and you have a static tabletop toy train setup in which the rolling stock goes round and round, through a number of switches effectively—but not realistically. Surround your mechanical aspects of the railroad with good basic or even simplified scenery and you are approaching state-of-the-art realism, which is what true model railroading is all about.

Most railroad model buffs who have tackled and overcome more complex engine kit and rolling stock kit building (as well as complicated electrical work) will find scenic and visual effect construction a breeze—so simplified that even the beginner can be rewarded on basic initial ventures.

The processes and techniques explored and delineated within the forthcoming pages are within the capabilities of the average person. Various approaches and materials utilized will be old hat to some, but their applications may be varied and novel. The techniques illustrated are basically my own, but I'm sure many individuals can expand on them, creating unique personal effects. A lot of my approaches evolved by studying the work of some of the masters, namely John Allen and Bill McClanahan.

All the working materials recommended and presented may be readily obtained by visiting the local hobby or art supply house. If none are in the local area, try mail order.

You will find that inclusion of basic do-it-yourself scratchbuilt scenery will be inexpensive as well as rewarding, expanding the realistic aspect of the pike whether small and concise or large and panoramic.

Chapter 1

Tools and Materials

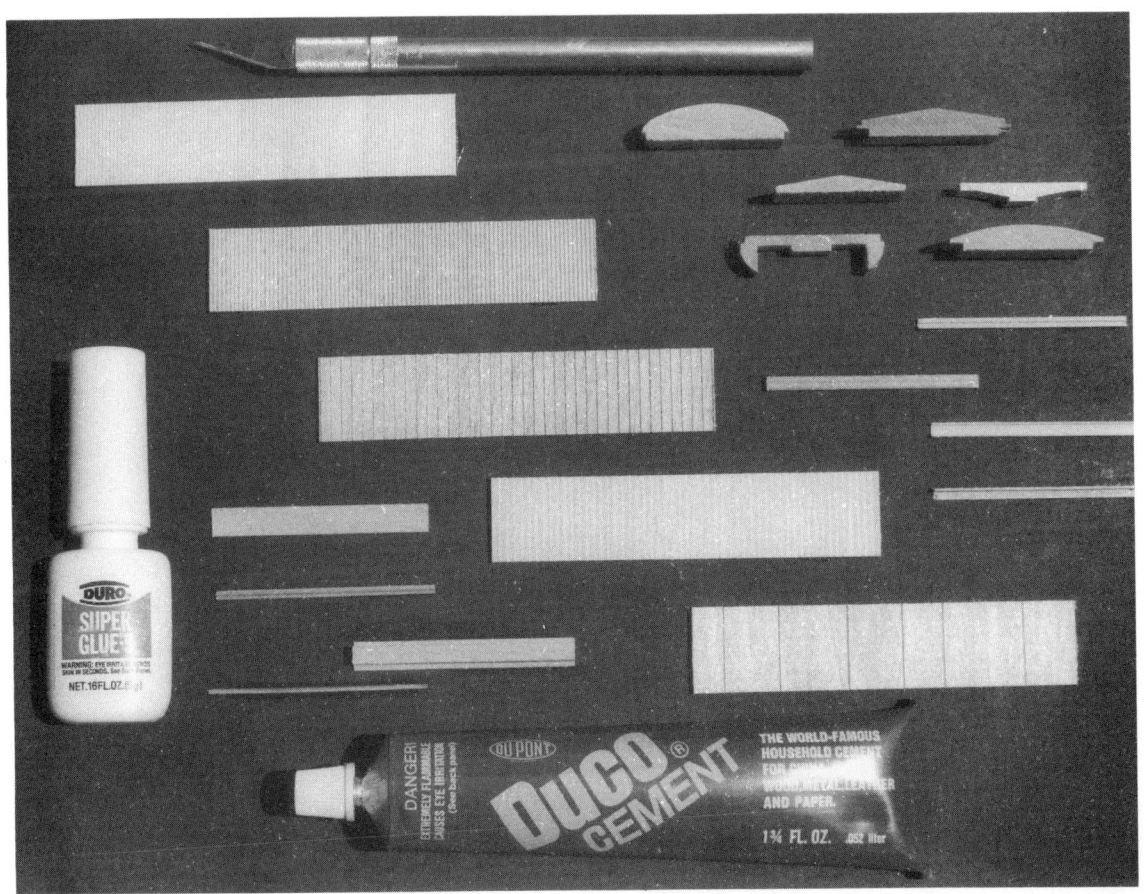

In scenic construction, scratchbuilding, and superdetailing, proper and adequate tooling plus a knowledge of what materials to apply to specific situations are a must. Here we will discuss basics, keeping tooling to a required minimum and materials confined to those applied to the situations encountered in this book.

Two basic tools no model railroader should be without are a Dremel Motor Tool and an electric soldering iron (Fig. 1-1). Dremel markets three versions; any of them will serve the purpose for the projects in this manual. For soldering, the Weller 8200 or equivalent model electric gun is highly recommended and is extremely useful in brass construction fabrication, wiring, and in track and turnout construction—both kit and scratch. With the soldering tool we must also include a good resign core solder and a can of flux.

Next on the required tooling list is a good pin vise for exacting hand drilling of minute holes in castings, superdetailing fittings, wood, styrene, etc. (Fig. 1-2). A set of drill bits from size 61 to 80 (decimal equivalents .0390 to .0135) is also good to have; an excellent set in its own box index is available from General Hardware Manufacturing. Pin vise and bit kits by X-acto are also readily available from most hobby and model railroad outlets.

CUTTING TOOLS

Cutting tools are minimal and fairly inexpensive for the projects entailed in model railroading. A good

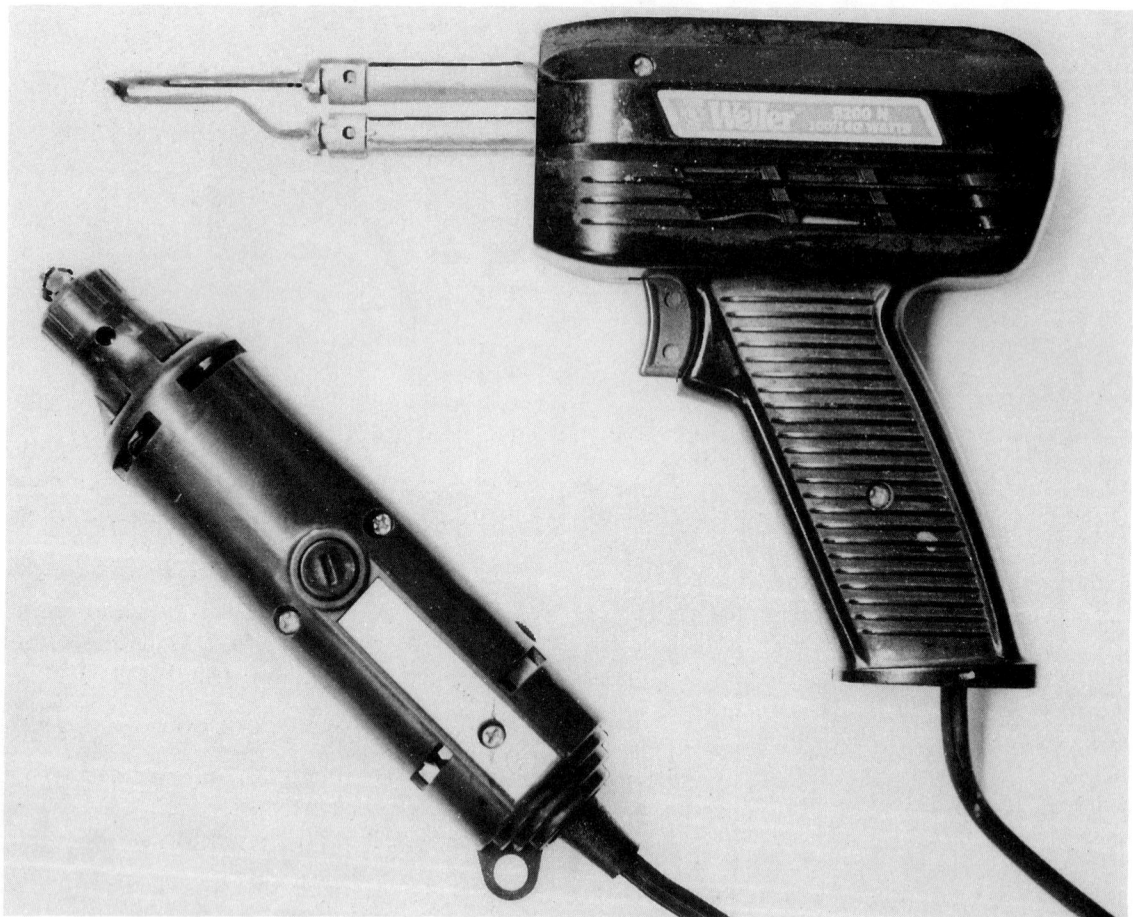

Fig. 1-1. Two construction backbones are the Dremel Tool and a soldering iron.

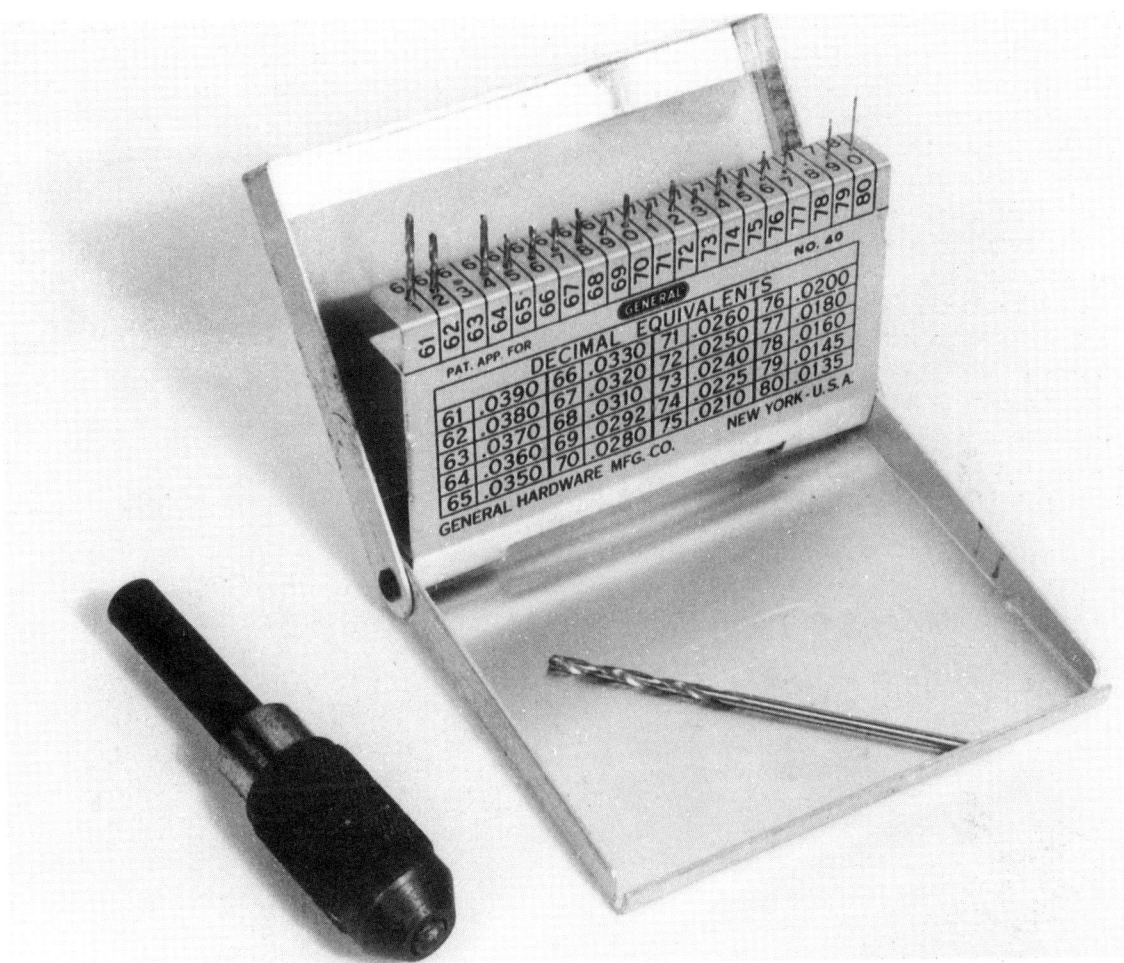

Fig. 1-2. Another common necessity is a pin vise for minihole drilling.

razor saw is essential, preferably a fine-toothed one. The X-acto No. 239 is ideal for all functions involving straight line cutting. A razor saw is also ideally suited for cutting track and rail, which it does cleanly and precisely. A miter box to use with the saw is a handy additive and the X-acto No. 7533 (aluminum) is highly recommended.

No modeler should be without the X-acto knife handle and a generous supply of X-acto No. 11 blades. This blade-handle combo will handle all fine wood and cardboard cutting operations and will also work adequately with thinner plastics and styrene.

PLIERS AND TWEEZERS

I recommend the X-acto No. 7485 cutting pliers for wire, rod, etc. and the X-acto No. 7509 long nose for precise bending and forming operations (Fig. 1-3).

Tweezers are necessary for fine construction work and for handling minute parts or pieces. Here the nod goes to the X-acto No. 7337, a self-closing type that ensures a positive grip (Fig. 1-4).

MISCELLANEOUS CONSTRUCTION TOOLS

The following are good to have on the construction tool roster even though they may apply to scattered or specific situations (Figs. 1-5 and 1-6):

- Jewelers Saw
- Needle file set
- Block sander

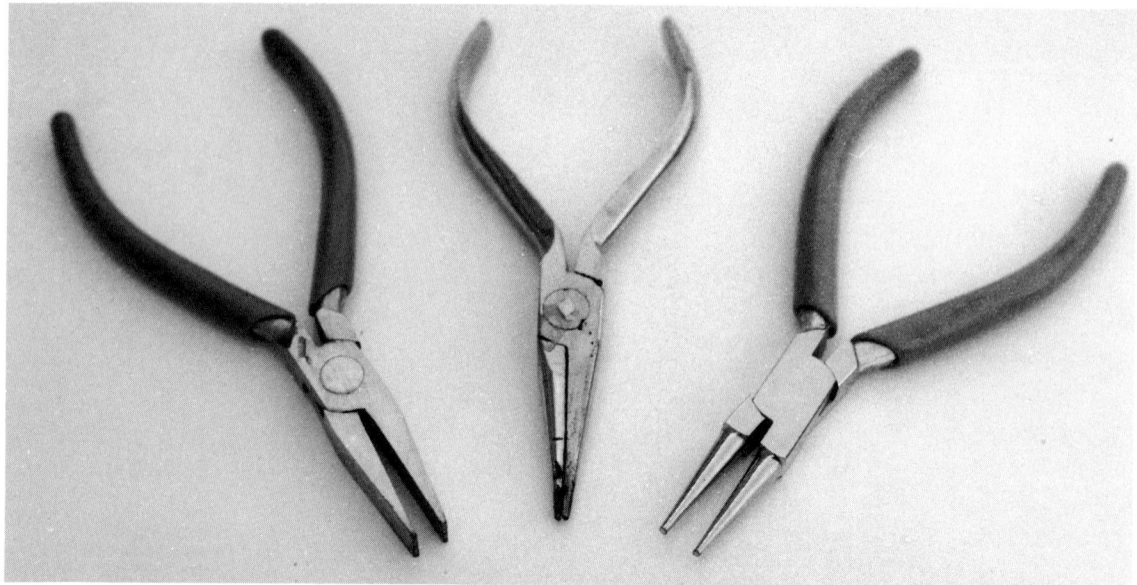

Fig. 1-3. Three handy pliers are (left to right): the X-acto flat-nosed, long-nosed, and snipe-nosed types.

- Jewelers screwdrivers
- C-clamps

BUILDING MATERIALS

Scenic

For modeling rocks, hills, tunnels, and terrain, the best and constantly used material is plaster of paris. This common household medium is readily available at all hardware and home construction outlets. It is also inexpensive and durable.

Another useful material for rocks is Bondo or automotive body filler. This is far more expensive than plaster of paris but in some applications is highly desirable. It is strong, chip resistant, light, easy to model and work, and takes paint well. Auto body filler can mainly be found in auto body supply houses. A working solution is created by mixing the stock filler with a hardening catalyst. The catalized putty solution must be used right after it is mixed because it sets and hardens within minutes.

For modeling water the best accepted medium is liquid casting plastic, also a two-part solution. Casting plastic is available at hobby and art supply shops (Fig. 1-7).

Structural

Wood. For buildings and a major portion of rolling stock, you can't surpass wood for ease of construction and detailing. The photo on page 1 displays the necessary equipment: X-acto knife with a No. 11 blade, super glue, cement, and milled and scribed wood. Balsa wood ideal for planes is too soft and brittle for model railroad specs. Cherry and mahogany can be used but are harder to work and cut. The accepted standard for railroad structures, roll-

Fig. 1-4. The X-acto cross action self-tightening tweezer.

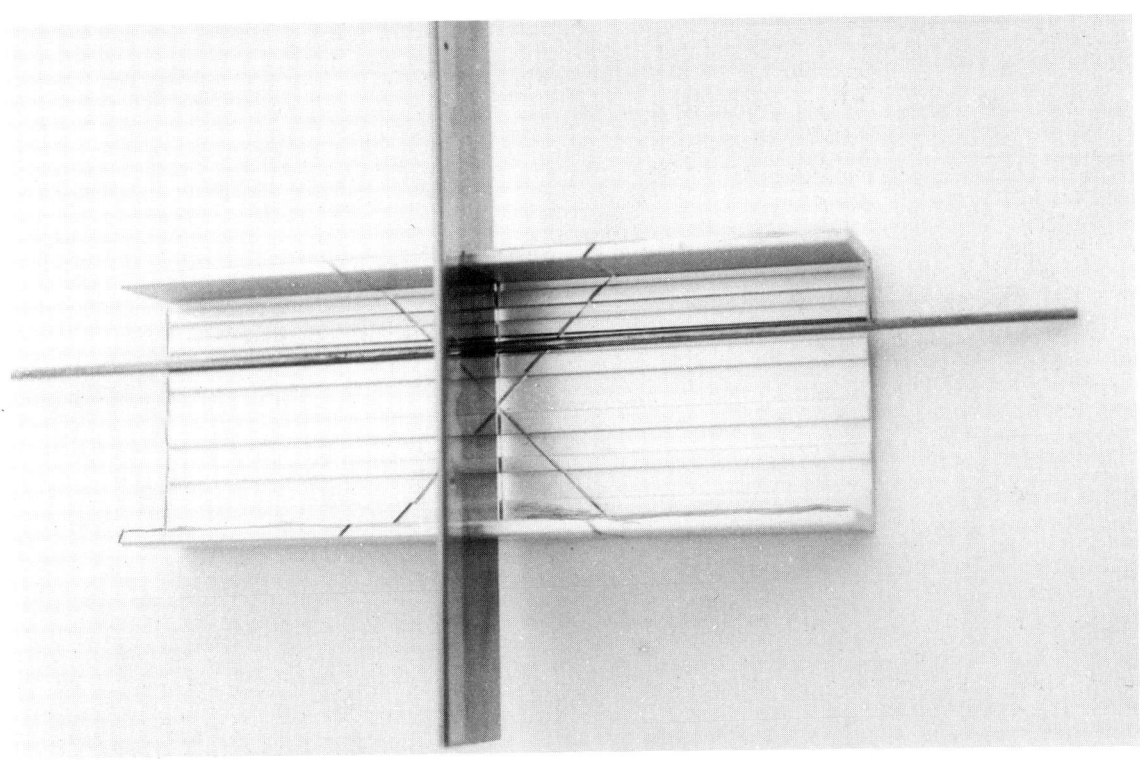

Fig. 1-5. Miter boxes such as this aluminum model by X-acto assist greatly in straight and angle line cutting.

ing stock, etc. is basswood. It cuts well, stains well, and sands well. It is sturdy and comes in scribed sheathing, a myriad of stripwood and structural material configurations, and is readily obtainable at most better hobby and model railroad shops. The only negligible shortcoming with basswood is its fibrous nature. It sheds slightly when cut and should be fine sanded. This hairy texture is present on the surfaces too, but this can be overcome with light shellac coating followed by fine sanding with 600 grit sandpaper (Tables 1-1, 1-2, 1-3).

Plastic. Plastic sheeting is also excellent for buildings and rolling stock; the most commonly used is styrene. Some plastic type materials are also textured to simulate stone, brickwork, siding, etc., making them well suited for creating textured buildings and facings. Most of the plastic materials marketed for model railroading application will cut well with a razor saw or X-acto blade, though not as easily as wood. Plastics and styrenes and durable and take paint well, provided the paint does not

have lacquer or acetone bases that tend to etch or melt the plastic.

Cardboard. The least popular of building materials—cardboard—can be efficient and desirable in specific situations when used properly. The best cardboard types are 1/16-inch illustration board and Bristol board. The latter is marketed in various thicknesses.

ADHESIVES

This chapter would not be complete without a few words about glue, since this is the agent that keeps everything together. Without adhesives model construction would not be feasible.

The two most common and widely accepted types are the super glues and butyl-acetate cement. Super glue is excellent for instant tacking application and is marketed by a number of glue manufacturers. The choice here is Duro Super Glue—simply because of its excellent dispenser with a pin type

5

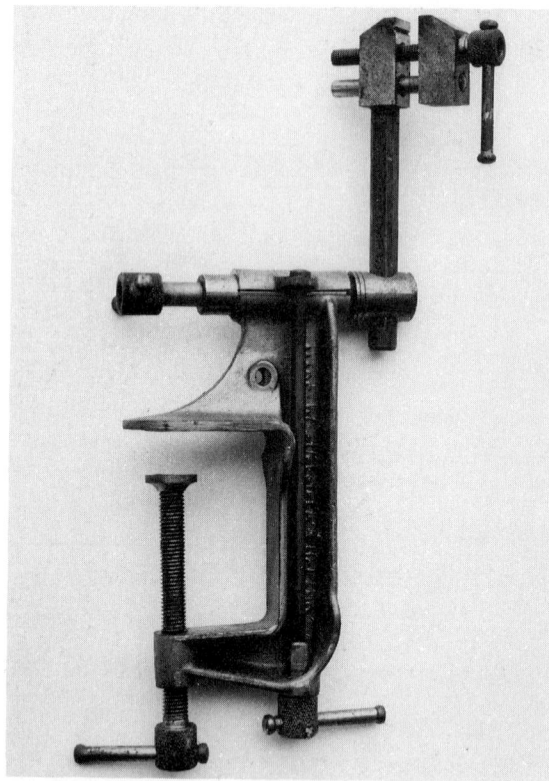

Fig. 1-6. A good instrument vise is handy for fine-modeling situations and holding smaller parts.

Fig. 1-7. Casting plastic is a two-part solution, unbeatable for water reproduction.

cap. All super glues are more or less the same and work well. For basic applications Duco Cement is the common denominator in modelmaking and works well with wood, metal, styrene, and cardboard.

For a specific situation such as grass and shrub adhesion, and securing ballast and shrubbery materials (grass, dirt, etc.)—rubber cement, Elmer's glue, and ballast cement will work best.

With the basics under our belts, we can embark on the following projects.

Table 1-1. Structural Basswood Shapes For HO Modeling.

(All wood is 22″ long)

SIZE (MM.)	SIZE (In.)
	1/32
1.0	.040
	3/64
1.5	1/16
2.0	5/64
	3/32
3.0	1/8
4.0	5/32
	3/16
5.0	.200
	1/4
8.0	5/16
	3/8
10.0	.400
12.5	1/2

Shape columns (illustrated): ANGLE, TEE, CHANNEL, COLUMN, I BEAM, ZEE, HAT SECTION, DOOR TRACK, FLANGE, CORNER POST

Perspective drawings labeled: Angle, Tee, Channel, Column, I Beam, Zee, Hat Section, Door Track, Flange, Corner Post

Courtesy Northeastern Scale Models

7

(All wood is 22'' long)

ROOFS AND FLOORS

OVERHANGING ROOF

RECESSED ROOF

CABOOSE ROOF

REFRIGERATOR ROOF

HOLLOW CABOOSE

INNER ROOF

FREIGHT FLOOR

END BLOCK

CLERESTORY PASSENGER

PASSENGER FLOOR
STREAMLINE ROOF

STREAMLINE FLOOR

MISCELLANEOUS CAR PARTS N

COACH SIDING with INTEGRAL BELT RAIL

CENTER SILLS
SOLID FREIGHT

N   HO   S   O

GROOVED

DEEP FISH BELLY

PASSENGER

ROOF WALK

LATERAL ROOF WALKS

BOLSTERS

⋈ **WINDOW MOLDING**

▭ **CORNER POST**

▭ **BELT RAIL**

▭ **THRESHOLD**

PASSENGER CAR BOLSTERS

PREFORMED GRABIRONS

HO Gauge 7/32'' Long
S Gauge 9/32'' Long
O Gauge 3/8'' Long

Please specify Roof Type when ordering floor.

EYE PINS

.018 Brass Wire
3/4'' Long
Eye Takes 1/32'' Wire

Courtesy Northeastern Scale Models

Chapter 2

Foundations for Model Terrain

(Courtesy Lauderdale Shore Line Model R.R. Club)

Starting from the ground up, the first factor to be dealt with in model railroading construction is the fabrication of the table or base from which all hills, valleys, and scenic structures evolve.

Table and tabletop construction choice is more or less left to the individual's amount of space, capabilities as a carpenter, available time, and expertise. Constructing a table is fairly easy, but lean toward a sturdy solid unit as opposed to a simple table slapped together for the sake of simplicity and economics. You can utilize existing tables, old tables picked up at rummage sales, ping pong tables, etc. The proper approach however, is a homebuilt, sturdy unit custom built to model railroad requirements. It should be simple, yet strong enough to maintain heavy structural units and scenery materials (wood, plaster, model railroad equipment, control equipment, etc.).

Because this book deals mainly with scenic and visual effects, I will delegate only a small portion to benchwork. This area has been covered thoroughly and frequently in magazines and is also covered in depth in other books by TAB Books, Inc.

My preference for sound, solid, simple and basic benchwork leans towards the L-girder table construction technique (Fig. 2-1). L-girder construction technique is ideally simple, even for the red thumb carpenter. It is strong, owing its strength to the L-girders that firmly support straddling joist pieces to which the final table top sheet (plywood or Homosote) is attached. This method of table construction is fast, sound, and flexible; squared joints and other structural facets do not have to be geometrically precise. All connecting points are accessible, and the most practical feature is ease of dismantling for major changes, additions, or trans-

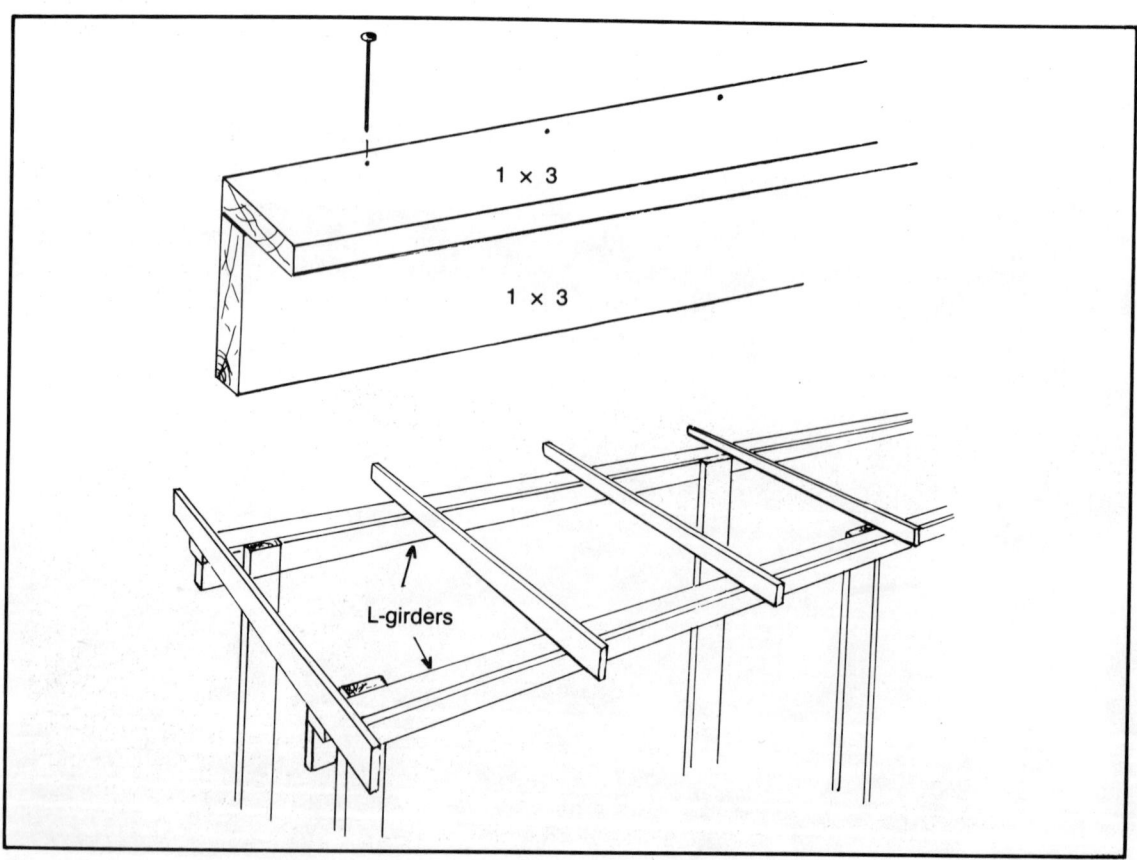

1 × 3

1 × 3

L-girders

Fig. 2-1. L-girder construction.

porting. If the proposed table work is large or lengthy, it is wise to cross brace the legs for added rigidity.

SCENIC FOUNDATION

Multilevel scenery (mountains, hills, etc.) is primarily achieved by building up from the tabletop. Gulleys, hillsides, and rock and mountain structures are modeled over a basic foundation that can be constructed of wood, cardboard, or screening—all of which are used in conjunction with each other to form multilevel terrain and structural scenic edifices. A framework is first constructed, over which groundwork and rockwork will be added and modeled according to the individual's desires and specifications. This must also conform to trackwork plans and coordinate with model environmental requirements. Pikes modeled on an Eastern theme are rich in greenery and shrubbery, and mountains heavily laden with trees. Rockwork is light to dark grey with intermittent overtones of warm brown. Western locales feature less greenery, the terrain is drier and often barren, unadorned but sharply sculptured rockwork is prevalent, rusty browns and earth colors predominate.

There are a few tried and true approaches to building up hills and mountains, which I label "groundwork." Cardboard shapes (bashed and shaped boxes) interlaced with cardboard strips make a good base, but the approach is not as popular or as accepted as wood and wire screen. In the latter method wood blocks are used to elevate 1/4-inch plywood or Masonite if a hillside or raised level is to be constructed (Fig. 2-2).

Plywood contoured shapes may also be cut and utilized for varied landscape profile effects and mounted horizontally or vertically to form the elemental foundation. Once the initial framing is complete, wire screening may be crumpled, shaped, then tacked or stapled into place (Fig. 2-3).

The wire screening used here is the standard metal or copper screening (window screening) readily obtainable at hardware stores. This screening is also available in plastic—which is not applicable in this situation because the plastic screening will not bend, contour, or hold its shape. Wire screen not only shapes well but also acts as a firm base over which terrain modeling mediums adhere to excellently.

SCENERY (TERRAIN)

Once the basic wood and wire foundation has been laid you are ready for texturing and modeling. Two basic mediums prevail in hard shell surfacing: Hydrocal and plaster of paris. Hydrocal is a newer, very hard plaster marketed by U.S. Gypsum and

Fig. 2-2. Screening and framework: the initial step to building hills and mountains.

Fig. 2-3. Screening is crumpled then tacked to supports.

very popular among scenery modelers. It is good but my nod goes to the old standby plaster of paris, which does everything Hydrocal does while being easy to find and use, and cheap. It also models easily and well. If you plan to include portals or culverts, add them before plastering (Fig. 2-4).

Once the wire framework is in place, you can fabricate the ground shell. Shellwork or basic plaster basing work can be done using a heavy plaster mix applied over the screening, or by an even better method as shown in Fig. 2-5. Plaster alone, if not thick enough, will sift or fall through the wire

Fig. 2-4. Place portals or culverts prior to plastering.

Fig. 2-5. To build up a good base newspaper is dipped in liquid plaster then draped over wire framework.

screenwork. In order to prevent this, mix the plaster to a heavy consistency using more plaster than water to attain a pasty state. In this mode however, the plaster will have to be worked smooth, which is not too easy because the heavier mixture tends to be rough in texture. A thinner plaster mix (with more water content) tends to flow out evenly.

Because ground texture varies between smooth and rough states in nature, these two contrasts should also apply in terrain modeling for added effect. To get a smooth shell effect, I found the following procedure to work best: First mix a plaster solution to a consistency like free-flowing pancake batter. Add a few teaspoons of white vinegar to slow down the setting of the liquid plaster mix. Then dip newspaper sheets into the liquified plaster, fully saturating the paper. Then, as in Fig. 2-5, place the newspaper over the wire screening and continue adding plaster-soaked paper until all the wire surface is covered.

A few words about plaster for the beginner who might not be familiar with its properties and mixing characteristics: Plaster is a soft rocklike material in its solid state. By soft I mean—not malleable, but easy to carve and detail, a process not easy on real rock. When manufactured, the plaster's water content is removed, leaving the plaster mix in a powdered state. To use the plaster or to allow it to revert to its natural rocklike texture, add water, mixing the two together until pasty. According to the amount of water added, the mixture can be loose like pancake batter or thicker and formable like soft clay. Whether it is mixed thick or thin depends on the use for which it is intended.

When working or applying plaster, the initial rule of thumb is to mix only what you need. Use it quickly before it starts to set. Once it gets past the creamy, spreadable stage it should be discarded.

The proper way to mix plaster of paris is to add the powder to the water, never vice versa. Stir continually while the plaster powder is added. Make sure all the lumps are broken down and mixed in until the solution reaches the texture of a heavy cream.

Remember, a thinner solution of plaster will flow when applied; in a heavier mixed state the plaster is more rigid and better to form and model. Do not be concerned if the plaster spread on the framework hardens before you can model it exactingly. It can be modeled and reworked in its hardened state easily with hand or motor carving tools. In fact, super or fine detailing (in rockwork) is best performed on the plaster in its hardened form.

To retard setting time and increase modeling time, always mix the solution using cold water. If you need a "quick set" solution, use warm or hot water. To further inhibit the plaster from setting up quickly, add 1 or 2 teaspoons of vinegar as you are mixing.

Plaster takes between 20 and 30 minutes to properly set before it can be worked and modeled. If some plaster is left in the bag, make sure you seal it well because it is susceptible to moisture. Store unused plaster in plastic bags or, if possible, metal containers.

COLORING AND PAINTING PLASTER

Although this is the final stage of scenic work, I will touch upon it now, due to the fact that some of the coloring methods must be instituted at a stage where the plaster is still liquid, or is close to hard stage.

Using pre-tinted plaster will save a lot of time. It will make the finished surface colorfast and, if scratched or chipped, will not reveal white marks. There are a number of water color solutions available (tube, bottle, or cake) but most will not work well. They are not available in large enough quantity to make a significant color change, for example, in a 5-pound working solution of plaster.

The best coloring solution I have found is fabric dye. It is inexpensive, easy to use, and very compatible with liquid plaster. The brand names to look for in fabric dye are Tintex or Rit; they are readily found in department stores and supermarkets. The colors you need are browns, tans, black, and orange. The browns and tans are the basic earth col-

oration, and black a good darkening agent. The orange (used moderately) is a good color tinting agent to work with browns and tans, especially if a Western terrain where the earth tones tend toward reddish and rusty tints is chosen.

Tinting the plaster mix provides an excellent base color coat, but the final hardened plasterwork must still be painted or highlighted with harmonizing colors to intensify physical scenic contours. Keep in mind that adding Tintex (working solution should be 1 teaspoon fabric dye to 1 pint of water) will speed up setting, so don't forget to add the vinegar and to work quickly. Color tinting or gradation is up to the individual; experiment until a desired base color is realized.

If you don't wish to pre-tint the plaster, overpainting the plaster is the other alternate. Here flat, water-soluble Latex (household type) paint is strongly recommended. If possible, paint just after the plaster has attained its "set," because the paint will work into and be absorbed by the plaster. This is almost like the "al fresco" technique of the Renaissance artists: these artists painted over fresh plaster in order to realize permanence of color, since the drying plaster absorbs the moist color and allows it to infiltrate the surface.

Latex paint has gained much popularity in model railroad scenic application. It has less of a tendency than turpentine-based paints to flake off over a long period of time. The newer water-based mediums seem to grip and adhere to the plaster better, working their way into all nooks and crevices. Also, if sawdust, turf, or earth texture material is dispersed over wet Latex, the paint when dried will firmly and permanently retain these materials. Thinned out to a watery consistency, Latex can be used as a "wash" around rockwork—seeping into the crevices to add modeling and dimension to irregular stone surfaces. Though Latex paint is water soluble in its working state, once it has hardened and dried it is impervious to water or other coloring agents that might be applied over it.

Other Coloring Mediums

I'm sure most of the readers will agree that the overall Latex basecoat is the ideal starting point for creating scenic color. The following coloring agents are added for color texturing, highlighting, and shadowing, and are applied either in a thinned-out "wash" state or are "drybrushed" on (as explained below).

Acrylic (Tube Type). Artist's acrylics are somewhat similar to Latex paint, also water soluble. In fact, they can be intermixed with Latex or used as tinting agents to alter earth base colors. Tubed acrylics have a fast-drying nature that can be beneficial in some situations, detrimental in others.

Occasionally I will use acrylics for a wash, where I thin down the color to a watery consistency, then brush it onto modeled groundwork or rockwork and allow it to run into ruts, crevices, etc. In the pockets, the wash will build up color or shading, which serves to heighten and dimensionalize the modelwork. I usually use darker colors (brown, black, grey).

Acrylics are also excellent for "drybrushing" and color modeling effects. Drybrushing is a scenic highlighting technique unique unto itself, and is used often for coloring and highlighting scenery. The process is simple: a dry brush is dipped into undiluted acrylic paint then worked back and forth (in a painting motion) over a paper or cardboard surface until the paint has worked its way into the bristles and has almost completely dried. In this semidry state the brush is wiped across the textured area(s) to be highlighted. The degree or depth of color highlighting depends on how much color is in the brush and the dryness of the paint. Drybrushing is an art and should be experimented with prior to finalizing scenic textures. When drybrushing with undiluted acrylics, work quickly because they dry rapidly.

Artists Oil Colors. Artists oil colors are especially effective as stains. They are diluted with turpentine or mineral spirits, or can be used in stock state. Oil colors can be worked the same way as acrylics, but they have two added advantages: they are slow drying and blend excellently. Because this color medium takes a while to dry it can be worked, blended, or re-worked with a dry or a turpentine-dampened brush or rag. Unusual highlighting effects can be obtained by applying a heavy wash over the surface of rockwork or textured plaster (earth shell), then wiping a rag (turpentine-dampened or dry) over the high spots in a fashion akin to antiquing.

For more subtle shading and color blending, airbrush painting is highly recommended. The use and application of the airbrush is covered further in Chapter 10.

Final Painting: Scenic Detailing

The trick in scenery painting and blending is to apply washes and coloring so that they flow and blend together in order to harmonize in varying hues. A wash or stain must never be heavy or opaque so that it looks painted on or unnatural, which can easily happen when creating artificial counterparts of natural scenery. Consecutively applied thin coats slowly worked up to the desired coloration are better; an area too light can always be darkened, but one that is color saturated cannot be lightened. Clean the brush frequently with the necessary thinning medium to keep it from becoming too heavy in color content. Experiment and get to know the various "earth" colors and how they best apply in various ground color situations.

The darker browns, raw and burnt umber and Van Dyke brown, are great for darkening and shading in straight form or as washes. These colors blend and work well singly or together. Adding a smidgen of black to these colors will also assist in shading and toning down color when required. The reddish brown colors raw sienna and burnt sienna also create some very attractive earth tones, especially in Western settings. Dark yellows and yellow ochre are very desirable highlighting and toning colors working well when blended into the aforementioned basic earth stains. Indian red used properly and in moderation can be added to intensify ground coloration particularly for Western and Southern environmental scenery where the soils exhibit hues predominantly red.

Experiment with color and stain combinations until you attain the degree of realism required for the environment to be modeled and recreated. Tables 2-1 and 2-2 will aid the neophyte scenic painter.

Table 2-1. Earth Colors And Hues.

Dark and Grayish Brown	Raw Umber, Burnt Umber, Van Dyke Brown (May be darkened with Paynes Gray or Black)
Reddish Brown	Burnt Sienna, Raw Sienna, Indian Red (Varying shades obtainable by adding Vermillion or Orange). The reddish browns may be darkened and shaded with Raw and Burnt Umber.
Dark Sand (Tan)	Raw Umber blended with a touch of Yellow Ochre. Tan and sand earth color can be shaded with a Raw Sienna wash, darkened with a touch of Raw or Burnt Umber.

Table 2-2. Rock And Stonework Stains.

Red and Reddish Brown Sandstone	Burnt Sienna alone or tinted with Indian Red
Yellow or Light Sandstone	Yellow Ochre tinted with Van Dyke Brown
Gray Granite	Thin wash of Paynes Gray highlighted with a consecutive wash of very dilute ultramarine blue.
Red Granite	Claret Wash followed by a very dilute Burnt Sienna Wash
Dark Gray (Basalt, etc.)	Heavy Wash of Paynes Gray streaked with dark blue-black (Ultramarine blue and lamp black), Drybrush highlighted with medium gray.

Note: These colors should be administered as wash stains, building up color intensity with successive applications.

MODELING ROCKWORK AND GROUND TEXTURE

Rocks

Good, precise rockwork always hits the eye and is the key facet in model railroad scenery. It must be well modeled and realistic in sculpture and coloring. In the preceding treatise we covered the color tinting aspects of stone simulation; now we will get down to the construction aspects.

The formation of rocks and boulders is best undertaken with plaster of paris because of its versatility. The plaster solution mixed expressly for modeling rockwork should be of a very heavy but malleable consistency, somewhat like very soft clay. It must not break down, settle, or run when put in place. If it is not firm enough, the strata marks and sculpturing cut into it will close up and

come together. If this starts to happen, wait until the plaster sets up a little more before shaping and sculpturing.

The procedure from start to finish is quite simple and can be rewarding even to the duffer. Once the plaster is mixed to the right consistency scoop it up with a spoon or putty knife and place it onto the ground base where it is to be modeled. Remember that in nature a rock, boulder, or rock face is an outcropping (unless a complete mountain is modeled), and following this principle it should be placed and modeled as an outcropping on a hillside or mountainside base.

While the plaster is still soft and workable, shape and model the rock to obtain the basic form and structure of the rockwork you are modeling. After the plaster begins to harden slightly begin carving in the rock lines and strata.

For modeling and texturing rocks, the best

tools are the palette knives used by oil painters. They are small, resembling knives or miniature trowels, and are ideally suited for modeling rock strata. A standard round-edged palette knife is good for applying the plaster and cutting the initial contours. A pointed (triangular) palette knife is better for finer cutting and grooving. For fine line and fine texture sculpting and engraving on plaster rocks, use an awl, X-acto knife (No. 11 blade) or small pen knife. Cut your lines in diagonal and horizontal random strokes but avoid "box line" or parallel grooving.

Your plaster rock formation might harden before you have completed your sculpturing. If this occurs do not despair; plaster can be modeled even in its hard state, though a little more effort is required. When I model rocks I consider wet sculpture a preliminary approach. To fine detail the rockwork after solidification, I use a Dremel tool with a fine engraving tip to execute the finishing touches.

Figure 2-6 shows a well-modeled and well-balanced rock outcropping. Note how the structural piece sits into the base as it would in nature. This rock was modeled with a round-nose palette knife, then detailed with a pointed palette knife and X-acto knife as explained previously.

Before undertaking rock modeling, study natural formations of rocks, mountains, etc. Both the beginning and expert modeler can learn much from scrutinizing natural rock formations first hand or in photographs. Keep in mind that proper modeling and texturing will have its effect on final painting and detailing. Thinned-out color and washes brushed on flow freely into the modeled cracks, lines, and crevices, and darken these texture lines. The higher relief images of the stone tend to be lighter. You can see how the wash technique serves two purposes in one step and is perfect for tinting rocks. With one application, both highlighting and shading is dispensed with.

When modeling a rock face, boulder, or outcropping on a mountain or hillside, the rockwork should appear to be part of its foundation and em-

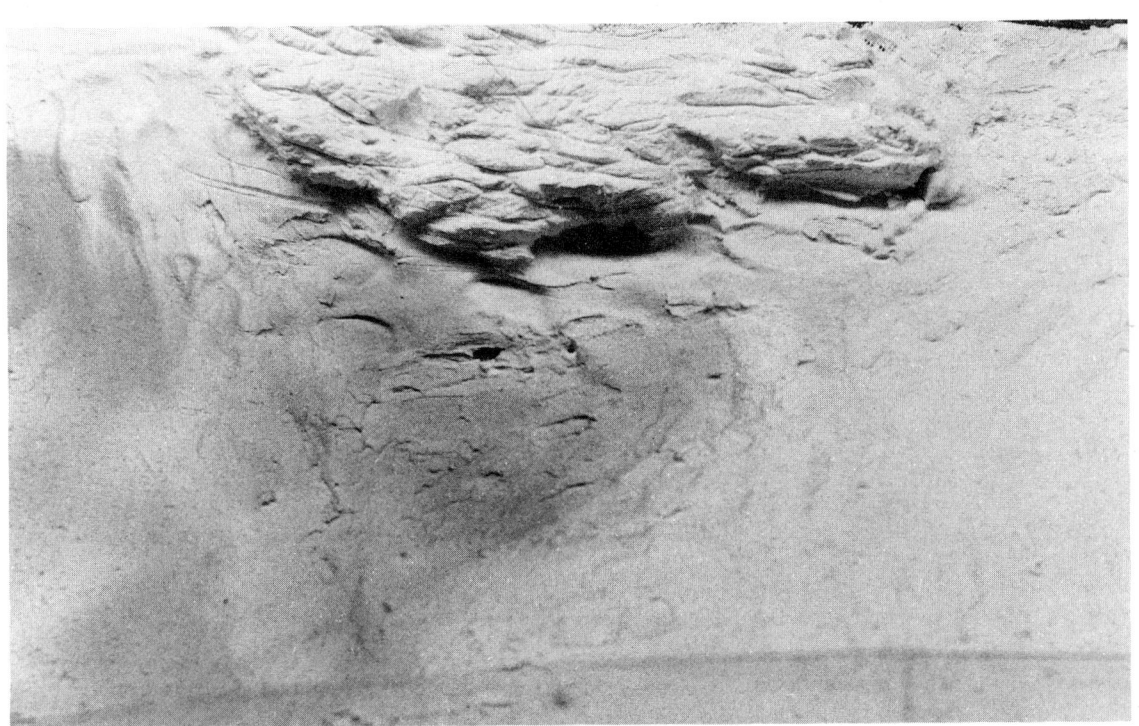

Fig. 2-6. Rockwork modeled in semidry plaster with a palette knife.

Fig. 2-7. Terrain surrounding rockwork may be smoothed over by hand or palette knife.

anate from it. Avoid setting rocks or boulders on top of a hill or hillside face as if they were performing a balancing act or defying gravity. Even segregated rocks or boulders usually have stone, broken stone bases, or some type of enveloping embankment to insure a solid foundation. Examples of this are presented in Figs. 2-7 and 2-8. In Fig. 2-7 note how the earthwork supports and serves as a solid base under the rocks, which are situated on a rather steep hill. Notice also how the earthwork around the rock has a smoother and contrasting texture to frame the rocks, allowing them to be more

Fig. 2-8. Rocks are colored.

18

prominent. The earthwork here was achieved by drawing the bristles of a 2-inch paintbrush lightly across the still-wet plaster shellwork.

Rocks should be painted utilizing two basic methods: wet washes and drybrushing, which we have described in a prior scenery painting section. Figure 2-9 shows stain wash being applied and Fig. 2-10 shows a completed, fully painted, and detailed rock formation. It is best described in one word: realistic.

Ground Texture

Ground texture assumes the next important role. Some feel that ground texture is more important

Fig. 2-9. After base coloring, a stain wash is applied over rockwork and allowed to flow into the nooks and crevices.

Fig. 2-10. A properly detailed, painted, highlighted rock formation.

than rockwork, but *both* are important, necessary, and must be utilized and coordinated into every model railroad pike—whether large or small.

Ground texture is exceedingly simple to model. It usually entails one simple step: adding or sprinkling on a ground texture medium, usually applied over a painted base prior to drying or with a brushed-on adhesive specifically designed to affix the ground texture material. This usually takes place after all the rockwork is completed and before trackwork is laid on.

Instant Rocks

A particular favorite method of rock formation and fabrication I came upon by accident while working in the automotive body repair field. The method is unique, foolproof, and above all simple and fast—hence the "instant rocks."

The material is automotive body filler, commonly referred to as "Bondo." Bondo is a two-part solution. The base is a plastic material that remains soft and pliable in stock state. The addition of a cat-

alyst, or hardener, converts the Bondo into a working solution that hardens after the two chemicals are united and intermixed. Once the hardener is introduced into the Bondo paste it must be mixed and used immediately, because the mixture sets in about five minutes. Proper mixing ratios and instructions are noted on the can. Bondo can be purchased in 1-quart or 1-gallon quantities and is available at all body shop supply stores. Don't plan on doing your entire layout with it however, since it is not cheap.

First you mix up your working solution, squeezing out a toothbrush-full amount of catalyst or hardener into a blob of Bondo about the size of a handball (Fig. 2-11). Bondo is grey or white. Vigorously mix the two together using a squeegee (Fig. 2-12). Whip up and mix the two solutions until the Bondo takes on the weak overall coloring of the catalyst. The catalyst is usually blue or brown. When the Bondo takes on the same but much lighter hue of the hardener throughout, it is ready for use. If streaks of the hardener show in the Bondo, you have not mixed the two thoroughly.

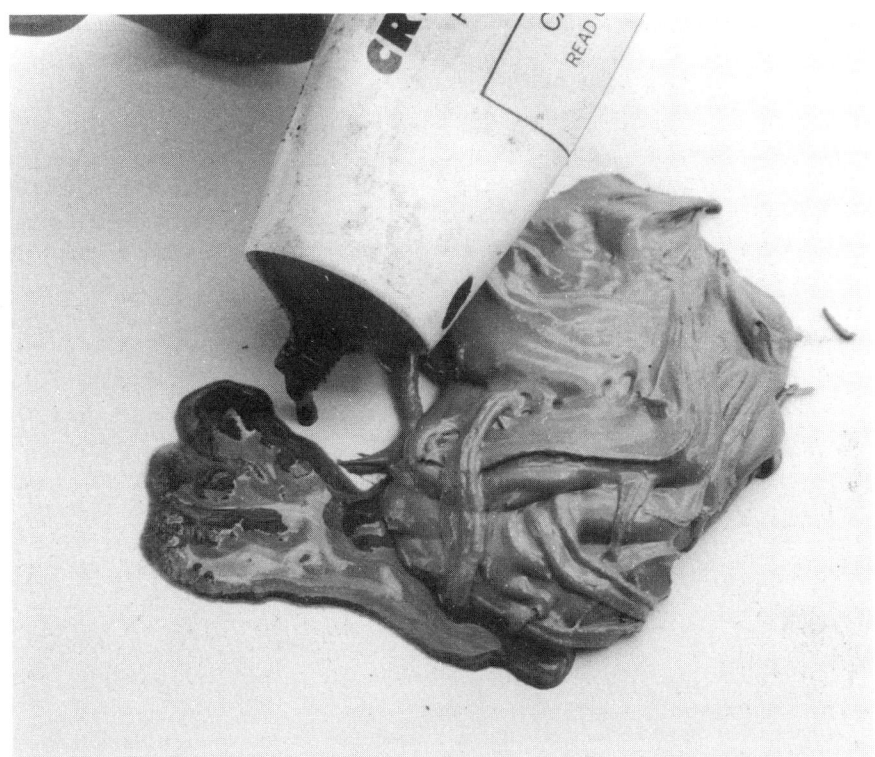

Fig. 2-11. Catalyst is added to the body filler material.

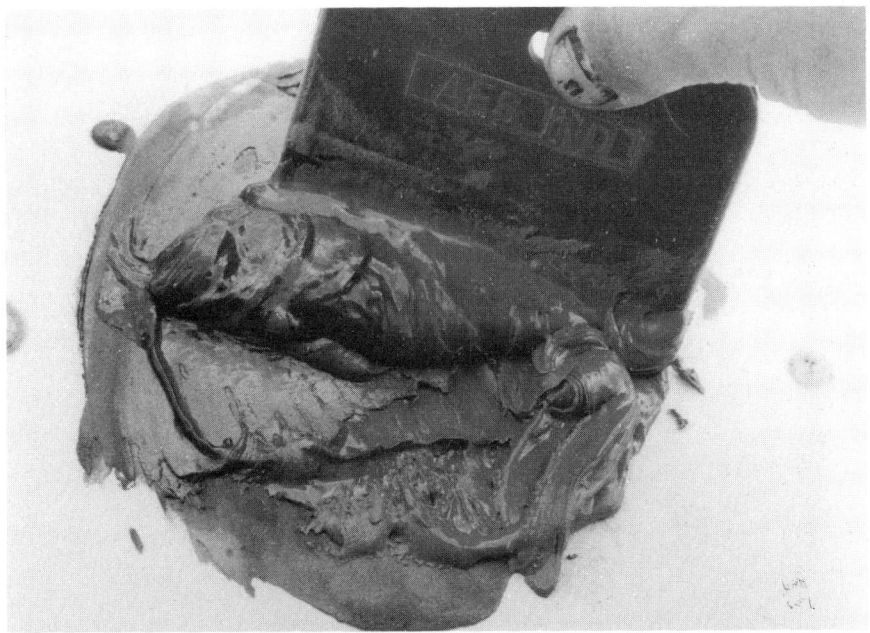

Fig. 2-12. The catalyst and filler are intermixed fully.

21

Properly mixed, the Bondo will be uniform in color throughout. Remember, a chemical hardening action is taking place so you must work quickly.

Lay up your basic rock formation (Fig. 2-13). About 10 minutes later, the basic form should be hardened and ready for final finishing. Then take a Dremel tool with with a fine grinder (Fig. 2-14) and cut in strata and detailing. Different size Dremel tool cutters and grinders can be utilized for different cuts and modeling, so you are not limited to any one tip. Many tips are marketed; find the ones best suited to your detailing requirements. The finished product is a rock formation, hard to distinguish from the real thing (Fig. 2-15). With this method you can turn out rocks on a production line basis. Bondo takes paint well, too, and its grayish coloring offers a built-in color base ideal for tinting and wash staining.

Ground texture should be as varied and contrasting as is found in nature. Use as many kinds of texturing materials and colors that are feasible, applicable, and indigenous to the environment on your pike. Grass or earth might predominate. Avoid a half and half ratio; be flexible. Above all, emulate nature in all instances. If you are using a lot of grass cover, don't make it all one shade of green; mix rather than match and work from the ground (earth) up.

Earth Texture

A number of earth texturing materials are available and work well. The simplest and most basic are coffee grounds, which are great for simulating dark brown earth. Used alone they are not as effective as commercial blends, but can be used in the proper situation.

Fig. 2-13. The malleable substance is formed to simulate a rock outcropping.

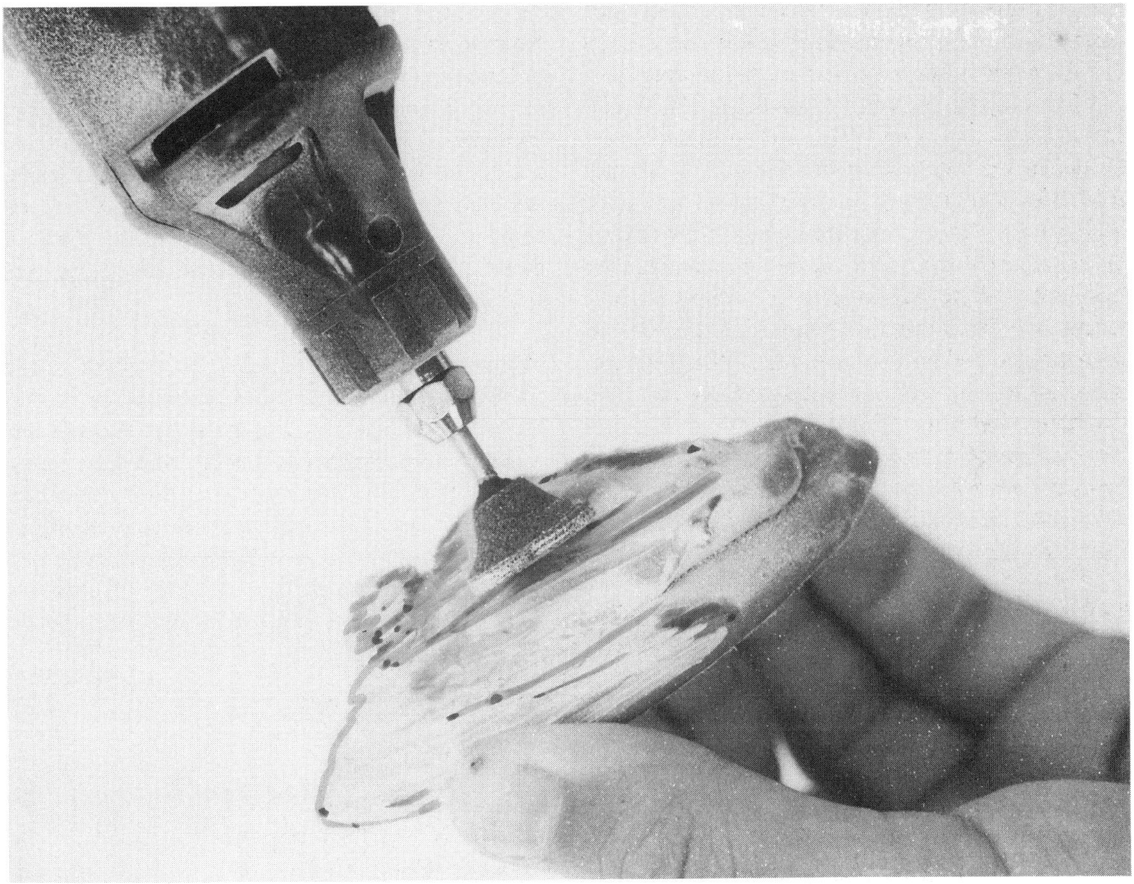

Fig. 2-14. Detailing and rock strata are added with a motor tool.

Fig. 2-15. The finished rock is ready for painting.

I have found that the best simulated earth coverings are those from Woodland Scenics. They are easy to obtain; the better model railroad scenic sources such as hobby shops carry the Woodland Scenics line. The Woodland Scenics earths I particularly recommend are the T50, T41, T42, and T60. The T50 is a very light yellowish earth color with a darker earth color intermixed. The T41 is the darkest of the earth colors and very fine in texture—good for Northern and Northeastern settings. The T42 is slightly lighter than the T41 but about twice as dark as the T50. The T60 is a medium brown, very coarse in texture.

These earth materials should act as the basis of most pike groundwork. Intermixing all or any two will give you further flexibility in achieving diversified ground cover. A proper application of ground cover is illustrated in Fig. 2-16. Here Woodland Scenics T60 earth was put to use. Its dark brown hue helps set off the rockwork on the hill.

Grass

Next in order of importance, working from the ground up, is grass. The mainstay for grass in model railroading circles is dyed sawdust. A lot of commercial grasses are marketed, but most of them are too garish or even in color. The best alternate is to dye your own. Sawdust can be readily obtained from lumberyards that sweep it up and throw it away. Most of the time you can have it for the asking.

To make realistic grass, dye various batches of sawdust different shades of green. Mix all the shades together and you will have excellent grass ground cover material. In this manner you can also control the color and make it either predominantly light or dark. One word of advice: don't use bright vivid Kelly green tints. Formulate the tints so that they are soft or dead greens since these look more realistic. Sawdust can be tinted with Tintex dye then dried out in the sun. Don't pick a windy day

Fig. 2-16. Woodland Scenics ground cover is excellent for groundwork texturing.

Fig. 2-17. Basic groundwork. This scene can be left as is or additional trees and shrubbery added. (Courtesy Lauderdale Shore Line Model R.R. Club)

to dry out your sawdust however, or your efforts will have been in vain.

High on the grass selection list are the commercial grasses put out by Woodland Scenics. They are widely available and easy to apply. There are four shades of grass plus a heavier grade called "coarse turf." Don't ignore combinations of turf and sawdust; the two make a dynamite yet realistic combination (Fig. 2-17). The next important facets in foliage are trees and shrubs; they will be covered in depth in Chapter 4.

TUNNELS AND TUNNEL PORTALS

Tunnels are in actuality "mountains with holes through them," but they add much color to a layout. What is a bona fide layout without a tunnel or two? Tunnels are modeled in the same manner as rocks and mountains, with an added touch: the tunnel opening or "portal."

A number of cast portals and portal kits are available and all are attractively composed of such materials as wood, plaster, or plastic.

Wood portals are very detailed and very colorful. My preference for a wooden portal is the one produced by Campbell Scale Models (Fig. 2-18). This portal is strikingly detailed and simple to put together—taking about 45 minutes of construction time. With its pre-fabbed parts and exacting instructions it goes together in a snap (Fig. 2-19).

Plastic portals such as the ones manufactured by Vollmer and Heljan are adequate, but to me they always retain a plastic look.

For portals emulating formal stonework you

25

Fig. 2-18. The Campbell Scale Models wood tunnel portal goes together quickly and easily.

can't beat the cast plaster types marketed by A.I.M. and Alexander. These castings are precise and very authentic-looking. They take paint, stains, and weathering highlighting very well. Plaster portals are simple to mount because they can be sunk into the adjoining plaster mountain terrain while the plaster is still wet. When the plaster is fully dried, the portal will be firmly affixed and sport a natural look.

Proper installation procedure commences by locating the proper position for portal placement. Portals should be located so that surrounding rockwork and scenery envelops the portal without interfering with adjacent trackwork.

Proper clearances must also be taken into consideration. According to NMRA standards (which

are correct) clearance from railtop to lower arch center point should be at least 21 feet 9 inches (scale)—or a minimum of 3 inches. The tunnel portal legs are usually long enough so that you will have leeway in mounting. You can also compensate by adjusting the height of the track roadbed. The track should go exactly through the center on a single portal. Double portals for dual tracks should be centered (at arch midpoint) over the centerline between the two tracks. Don't mount the arch higher than 2 scale feet (about 1/4 inch) more than the minimum clearance, or it will appear awkward or out of scale.

Painting or Staining the Portal

The best medium for plaster portals are oil stain

Fig. 2-19. When complete the Campbell portal makes an excellent and realistic model.

Fig. 2-20. An overall wash stain is liberally applied to portal for coloring.

washes. They cover and handle well and can be worked in easily. All you need to precolor the portal prior to mounting is one good stiff brush (1/4 inch) and one smaller detailing brush (No. 2 round sable is perfect). The tinting medium is oil coloring, the thinning medium is turpentine.

First formulate a wash or stain (about 1 part color to 5 parts turpentine). Then brush the stain quickly and liberally over the stonework (Fig. 2-20). Before the stain is fully dry, wipe it down as shown in Fig. 2-21, which serves to highlight the higher stonework. Consecutive stain coats may be applied, repeating the process until the desired coloring is reached. Once overall tonality is realized you can further highlight and detail individual portions of the portal with thinned-down zinc white oil color, using the dry brush technique (Fig. 2-22). After the painted portal is fully dried, age and weather it as advised in Chapter 10. Figures 2-23 and 2-24 show portals in place.

The following is a list of stone colors highly recommended for portal staining:

- Claret—heavy staining simulates red granite
- Lampblack—thinned to a weak wash simulates limestone.
- Van Dyke brown and orange—simulates brown sandstone
- Yellow ochre and Van Dyke brown—simulates yellow sandstone
- Burnt sienna and lampblack—simulates shale. For a warmer toned shale, replace lampblack with Van Dyke brown.

Fig. 2-21. Surface is wiped down to highlight the stone, while recessed crevices remain dark due to heavier buildup of color.

Fig. 2-22. Stonework is further highlighted using the drybrush method.

Fig. 2-23. A. I. M. dual tunnel portal in a mountainside setting.

Fig. 2-24. Another stone portal by Alexander shows good modeling and intricate stonework.

Chapter 3

Trackwork

(Courtesy Lauderdale Shore Line Model R.R. Club)

Trackwork almost never receives more than secondary consideration as a visual or scenic additive either from the casual or the dedicated railroad modeler. I, at one time, never thought there was much that could be done to track, save for laying it down neatly, evenly, and correctly. That is, until a few years ago when I attended a regional NMRA convention and scrutinized a custom-made turnout entered in the modeling contest that amazed me and enlightened me on the virtues of superdetailed track.

The turnout was exactingly built, exhibited no joining or solder marks, every fishplate was in place, the rail weathered and the ties realistically colored, weathered, and worn. Of course I would not advocate this type of an approach even for the more serious model railroader, since most of the glorifying would go unnoticed and trackwork detailed to this infinite degree takes more time than even the most dedicated buff is willing to devote. The average modeler will go just so far in track but the real purist nut can, if he wishes, take the superdetailing to its infinite degree and further heighten realism on the layout.

Railroaders have at their disposal a number of trackwork alternates from simple, slap-together snap track to the more sophisticated do-it-yourself, hand-laid track. The simple, piece-together sectional track is basically kid stuff; great for tinplate freaks, but it just doesn't cut it for realism or looks. Sectional snap track is best left to the children.

Flexible track such as the type manufactured by Atlas, Rail Craft, Peco, and Lambert is great for beginners and is not bad looking. The shiny plastic ties are well detailed and—if properly colored with Floquil flat brown paint and weathered—sometimes cannot be distinguished from handlaid trackwork featuring real wood ties. Flex track, available in 3-foot lengths, can be easily bent to conform to any desired radius while automatically retaining the proper rail to rail distance (Fig. 3-1). Rail Craft makes flexible track in three sizes: Code 100, Code 70, and even Code 55. The Rail Craft flex track is also excellent since its ties have an unevenness akin to prototype track and extra built-in details like tie plates and miniature spikes, which are hard to include even in hand-laid track. Lambert also produces some good-looking flex track mate-

Fig. 3-1. Flex track is a good alternative for the timid tracklayer.

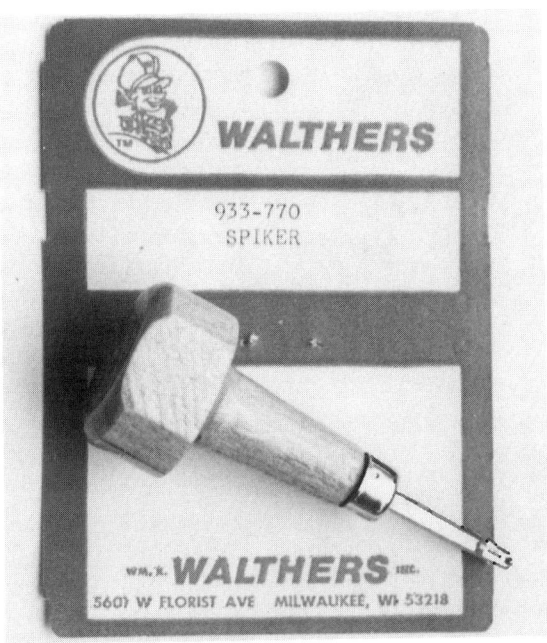

Fig. 3-2. The Walthers spike is a handy tracklaying tool and can be used for all spike sizes.

rial but in Code 100 and 70 only.

Rail size preference, whether in flex or hand track, is up to the individual. The smallest (Code 55) stock has the authentic fragile appearance of real railroad track but is actually too small for trouble-free operation of HO locomotives and rolling stock. The purist usually selects Code 70 rail; it is closer to scale in appearance, and is also functional. Code 100 rail is oversize scalewise and not very popular among true scale aficionados.

Though I am a stickler to perfectionism, in scale I tend to choose Code 100 since it is stronger, easier to work with, and simpler to lay and spike. In addition, it makes the locos and rolling stock traversing it less prone to derailing and mistracking—especially through switches. Unless locomotives have well-sprung drivers and narrow wheel flanges they might have trouble negotiating rail other than Code 100. For guaranteed better tractability of rolling stock I favor Code 100 rail, regardless of the type track laid down.

Two types of metal rail are also produced: nickel silver, and brass. Here, nickel silver gets the nod. It is more realistic in appearance (color) and does not tarnish or oxidize as readily as brass. The only plus factor with brass is its better electrical conductivity, which is a negligible feature (Fig. 3-3).

The other alternate to flex and hand-laid track is an excellent compromise between the two: Tru-Scale features milled wood roadbed integrating roadbed and tires. The rail is laid into notched ties, that situate and space the rails, that are then spiked into place. The roadbed is self-gauging, which take a lot of the sweatwork out of tracklaying. After the roadbed is ballasted and the rails spiked down, the trackwork takes on a most realistic look. In addition, Tru-Scale markets a variety of mounted and unmounted turnouts, crossovers, ready track, and various preshaped roadbeds for the do-it-yourself buff (Figs. 3-4, 3-5).

The epitome of fine prototypical trackwork is hand-laid track, which is comprised of rails, ties, and roadbed all assembled by hand. This approach consists of the assembly and treatment of its integrated parts—namely the roadbed, the ties, and the rail.

ROADBED

All trackwork is usually placed on roadbed (crushed rock and stone) in prototype situations, and this naturally must be duplicated in miniature. The only time roadbed is deleted in real life is on most sidings, yards, and in secondary trackage.

There are a number of ways to build up roadbed on a model railroad layout. First a base is laid down, consisting of cork, wood, preformed roadbed or Homosote, a material available at most lumber yards. Cork is not too desirable because it is smooth and uniform, hence unrealistic in appearance.

Pre-formed roadbed is ideal for the neophyte. Homosote is good (it holds spikes admirably) but it must be cut (it comes in 4- × -8 sheets) and the sides should be sloped. It is also about 1/2-inch thick, which I feel is too thick for a realistic-looking roadbed. Homosote is great as a tabletop surface and for yards that boast no roadbed. It makes a great base for ties, rail, and spiking.

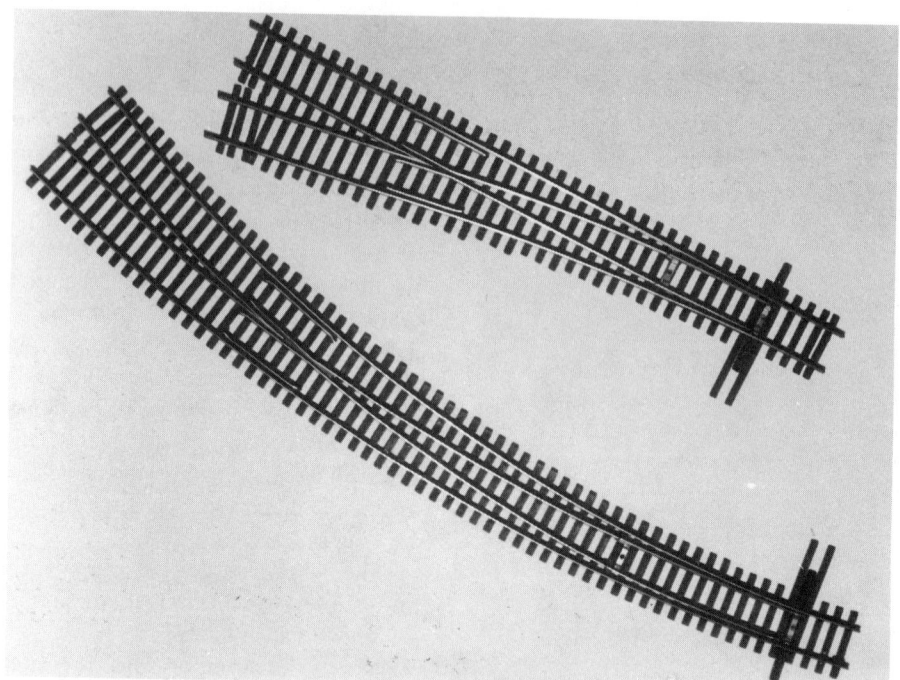

Fig. 3-3. Some typical commercial turnouts (nickel, silver, and plastic).

Fig. 3-4. Tru-Scale track offering feature regular or milled roadbed or tru-track. (Courtesy Tru-Scale)

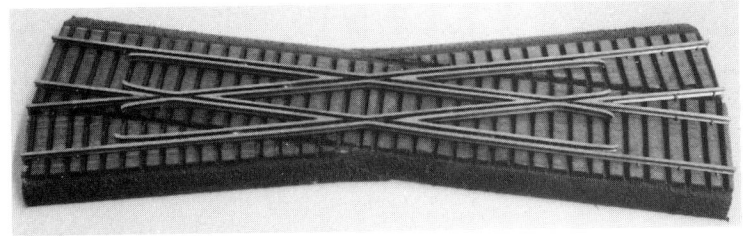

Fig. 3-5. The new Tru-Scale 14-degree crossover; neat and well detailed. (Courtesy Tru-Scale)

My favorite roadbed solution is basswood; I don't know many who go this route. I buy stock Northeastern basswood 1/8-inch thick × 3 inches wide × 22 inches long. I cut this down the middle, which gives me two pieces 1 1/2 inches wide. The 1 1/2-inch width cut stock serves as my roadbed base, which is nailed onto the table as in Fig. 3-6. To obtain the sloping sides I use spackle or filler placed with the finger as in Fig. 3-7. Curves and radii must be built up by piecing small sections, using this method.

BALLAST

Ballast is important and adds the finishing touch to trackwork. It is usually applied after the ties are glued down and before the rail is spiked on.

A number of ballast (stone) types are marketed in various shades of brown and grey. The ballast should not be chosen by the individual's color preference but the type needed for the situation. For instance; grey and mixed grey ballast is found in Northeastern U.S. locales. Southern and West-

Fig. 3-6. Northeastern basswood roadbed (see text).

Fig. 3-7. The edges are beveled with spackle.

ern coloring tends toward brown and iron ore coloration.

Don't choose ballast too rough or large in texture; it will look phony. For a true appearance use blended or multi-hued ballast, but make sure the intermixed colors relate closely in coloration. For sidings or yards use the finest ballast or powdery medium available and lay it flat. For securing ballast, a number of ballast cements are sold. The best and simplest adhesive I found was Elmers white glue, diluted one to one with water. The glue is applied by brush on the roadbed wood base and the ballast is then sprinkled on with a spoon or by hand. Excess unaffixed ballast can be blown off or dusted off with a soft camel hair brush.

TIES

In this area there also are a few certified approaches. The simple method is buying pre-cut, pre-colored ties. They come in a few thickness configurations and colors. I find the best and the most reasonably priced ties to be those made by B. K. Enterprises. They are precut and stained and can be found in the Walthers catalog along with all the fine B.K. Enterprise track line.

Do-it-yourself tie makers can save money (but not time) cutting their own ties from Northeastern basswood (1/32 × 3/32) which comes in 22-inch stock lengths. Some modelers might prefer a tie thickness of 3/64 inch, also available from Northeastern.

Working with raw wood means you must stain your ties—a simple feat. Floquil provides two stains well suited to tie coloring: walnut and cherry. My approach to tie staining is simple. I stain a handful of raw wood ties cherry and another handful walnut. A third handful I stain with a combined solution of one part cherry and one part walnut. I take the three colored lots and intermix the three in a common bag. This gives me a varying tie color effect that looks realistic.

Spiking down the rail is the final track construction step. Different size spikes can be obtained through hobby shops specializing in model railroad supplies. Choose a spike that is not too large or out of scale, yet strong enough to be easily driven into the roadbed base. Pros like to spike their rail using needle-nose pliers. The spike is grabbed between the teeth of the plier three quarters of the way up the spikes shank (near the head), then the spike is forced in till secure. Then the tip of the pliers (with the jaws closed) is used to drive the spike the rest of the way in.

An excellent spiking tool is the Walthers Spiker No. 933-770. This tool grips the spike (lined up with the thumb), starts the spike with hand pressure, then utilizes a grooved tip to finalize the driving of the spike.

A typical step-by-step track laying sequence is illustrated in the color section of this book.

WEATHERING TRACK

Prototype track is never clean and new looking, so why should model track be? Trackwork should be weathered, dulled, and rusted. Trackwork should take on a rusty, oil-stained (sporadically) surfacing, save for the rail tops that usually have a shiny metallic appearance, especially when subjected to constant use. Ties are usually laid crooked every now and then, exhibit cracks, and are sun bleached and grime stained. *Don't* overlook track weathering. It is just as important as structure weathering. A few sporadic weeds and vegetation between ties will also serve to heighten realism. Black, glossy enamel will emulate oil spills; rust and dust can be drybrushed or airbrushed on. Clear lacquer or clear nail polish can simulate water spots and puddles.

Rail should also be weathered. Floquil Rail Brown is the exacting paint medium for this. The best way to apply the Rail Brown coloring is with an airbrush. After the entire rail is sprayed (prior to spiking and mounting) the rail tops are wiped clean with lacquer thinner. The resulting appearance exactingly emulates prototype rail.

SWITCHES AND TURNOUTS

Switches and turnouts—necessary to even the simplest and most basic layouts—can be bought assembled or in kit form, or may be scratchbuilt. For purists, the latter approach is mandatory when specialized, out-of-the-ordinary turnouts are required. Though building turnouts from scratch is not a complex project, it is also not as simple as laying straight track. Rail must be cut and bent, frogs must be constructed, and built-in working mechanisms must be added.

Tie laying procedures for switches differ only in the respect that in a turnout the tie configuration progressively expands in length as the curve comes out of the straight section. For turnouts, special ties may be obtained that are excellent and contain specific, illustrated instructions on construction (Fig. 3-8). Campbell Scale Models markets raw wood turnout ties and B. K. Enterprises offers an excellent special turnout package of prestained ties. Figure 3-9 shows the differing factors in ties laid for turnouts and ties laid for straight track.

Building turnouts from scratch is not too difficult, and is the most economical way to go. All you need is a supply of rail, ties, a good soldering iron, wire cutter or zona saw, spikes, a needle-nose pliers, and a good file. Illustrated in this chapter is the favored approach of Paul Voelker, a member of the Lauderdale Shore Line R. R. Club. Paul, an expert in tracklaying and fabrication, builds all his trackwork in Code 70 rail, closely following Union Pacific prototype specifications.

A great many custom turnout fabricators advocate building a turnout from the frog out, that is, constructing the frog section first. This allows great flexibility because the consecutively laid outer rails can be jockeyed about to achieve rail spacing. This is a lot easier than constructing the inner frog after the outer rails are laid. This is a great method when you are building standard turnouts such as No. 6, No. 8, etc.

Voelker's turnouts may be 6 1/2s or 7 1/2s. For these oddball turnouts, a Voelker finds it is easier to lay the outer rails, followed by exacting meas-

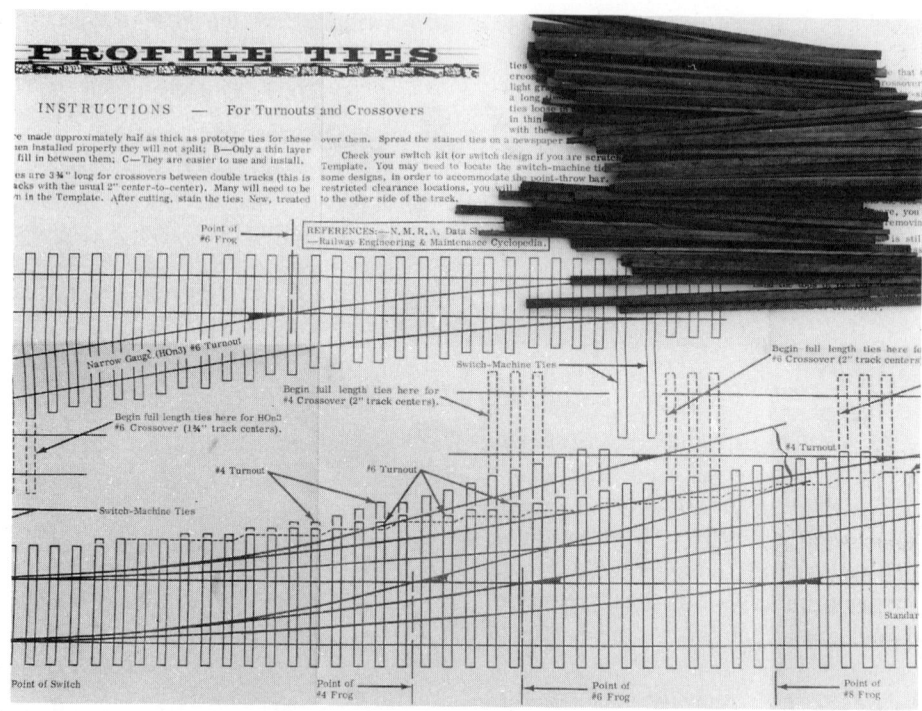

Fig. 3-8. Ties for switch building are a Campbell Scale models specialty.

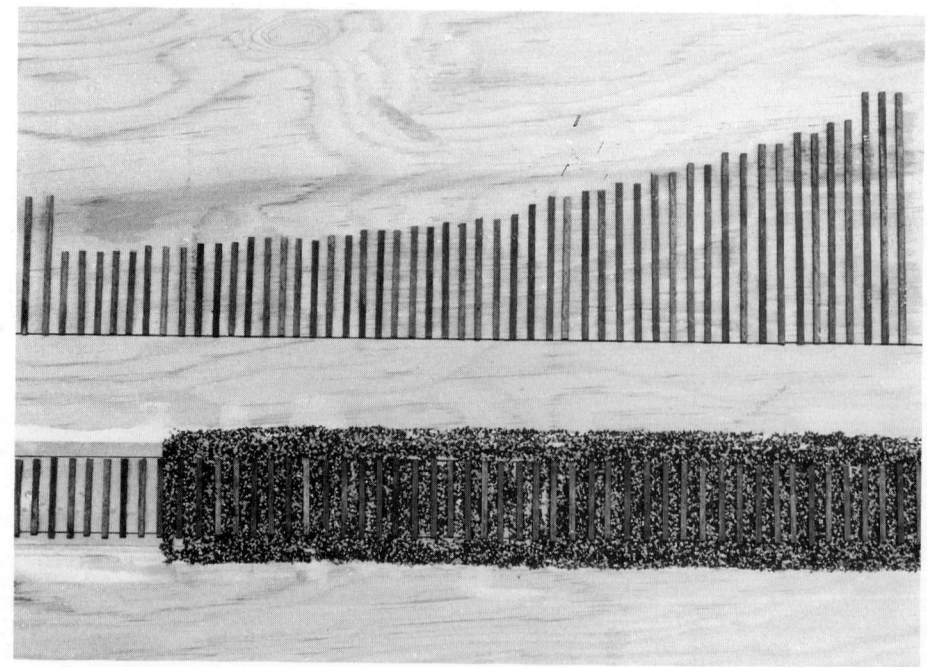

Fig. 3-9. Regular tracklaying procedure vs switch tracklaying procedure.

urement procedures and measurement planning in order to construct the frog.

There are a number of track gauges available; the pros tend to favor the three-point gauges, which afford better and more critical spacing in track and turnout construction. Two typical gauges of this type are the Kadee Multi-Purpose and the Model Die Casting units.

Here in a nutshell is Paul Voelker's approach to turnout construction, which I feel is a very valid and exacting one: First, the outer rails are located and spiked. The gauge and ruler are carefully implemented so that the consecutively placed rails and frog will fall into their proper place (Fig. 3-10). The first frog point rail-piece is then added; spacing carefully checked with the three-point gauge (Fig. 3-11). In Fig. 3-12 we see the second frog point rail placed, spiked, and secured. Voelker spikes his rail down using the needle-nose plier method mentioned previously in this chapter. The frog point is then soldered using a modelers soldering iron (Fig. 3-13). Surface irregularities that may manifest themselves due to over-soldering can be finished off and evened out with the aid of a small modeler's file.

The remainder of the frog is now assembled. The end of the frog rail is kinked slightly about an inch from the end (Fig. 3-14), then situated in its respective place with the aid of a track gauge to check spacing, height, etc. The final frog rail is positioned (Fig. 3-15) and then spiked and soldered into place. The frog piece must then be grooved and excess solder ground out so that wheel flanges will traverse the frog without jumping out or derailing (Fig. 3-16). Guard rails are now added (Fig. 3-17). Fig. 3-18 shows the point section. Rail points must be filed and tapered *before the rails are spiked down*. Filing prior to spiking is critical and must be frequently checked until the proper taper angle is achieved.

For those modelers not too proficient with a soldering iron or the exacting alignment procedures necessary to construct turnouts, excellent turnout kits and pre-fabbed frog sections are made available. A number of these can be seen in the Walthers catalog. These kit components are produced for standard turnouts only (No. 4, No. 6, No. 8, etc.). The finest frog assemblies are the ones produced by B. K. Enterprises of Rice Lake, Wisconsin. You can obtain the frog sections alone (assembled) or the frog and point section as a complete unit (see Fig. 3-19).

These pre-fabbed components are mounted

Fig. 3-10. The outer rails are laid first in odd degree turnouts.

Fig. 3-11. Building the frog commences.

Fig. 3-12. Another frog rail is spiked down.

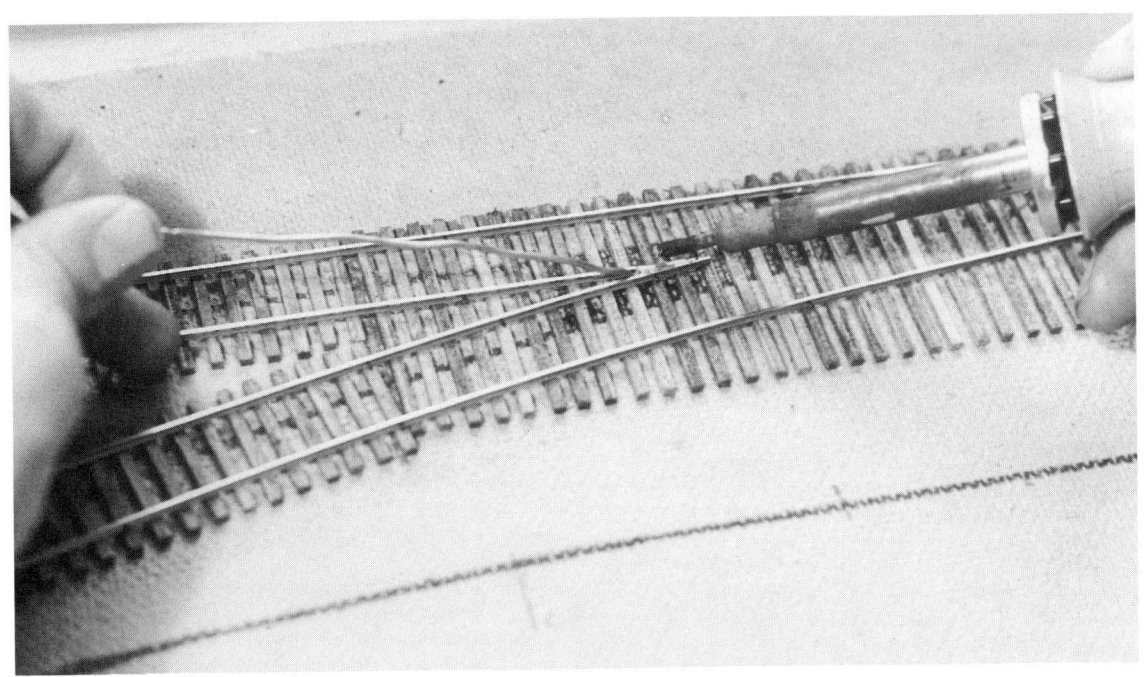

Fig. 3-13. Initial soldering takes place.

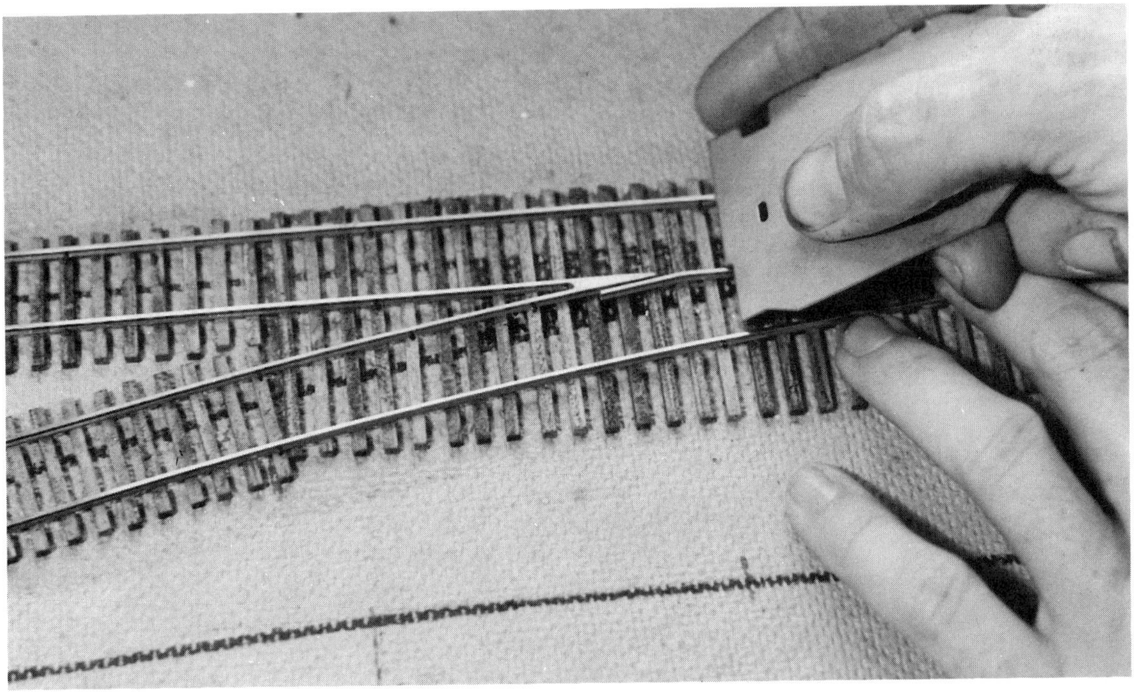

Fig. 3-14. Corrective measurement is taken as one of the movable frog rails are placed.

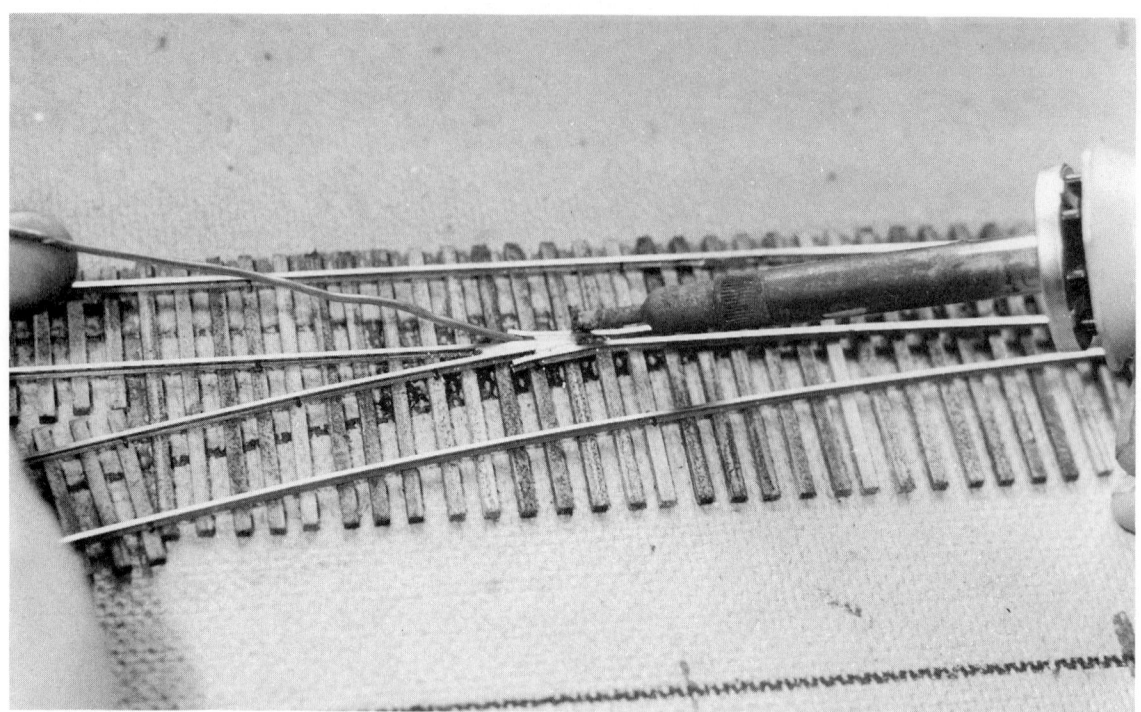

Fig. 3-15. Second point rail is soldered in place.

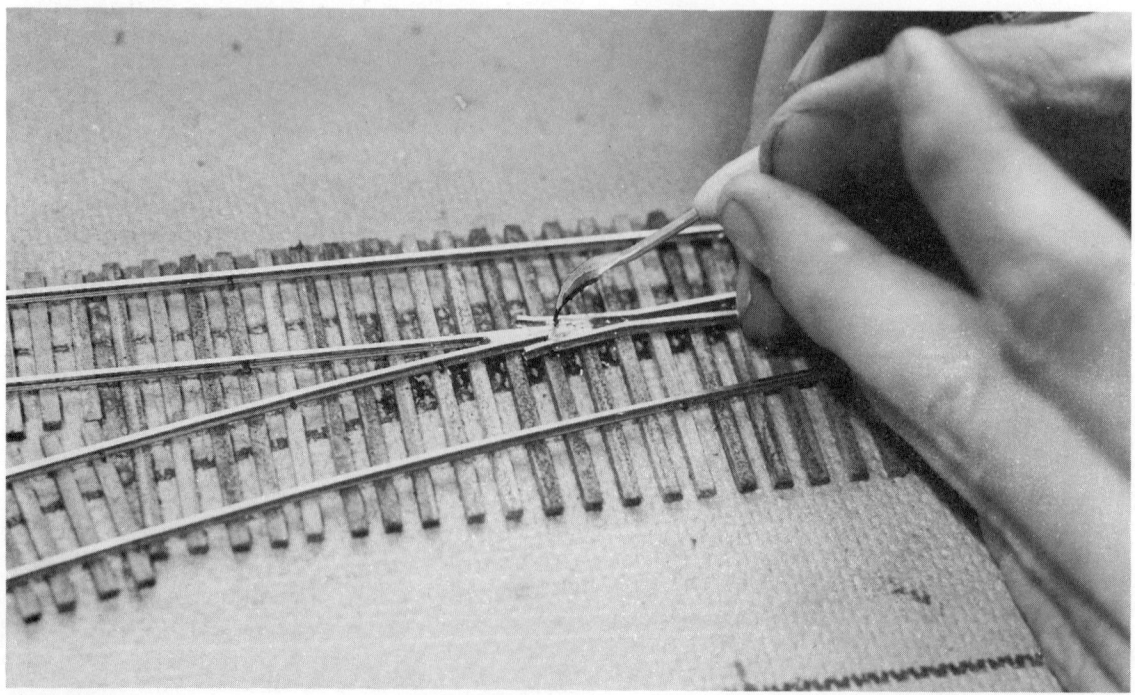

Fig. 3-16. Excess solder is scraped away from frog assembly.

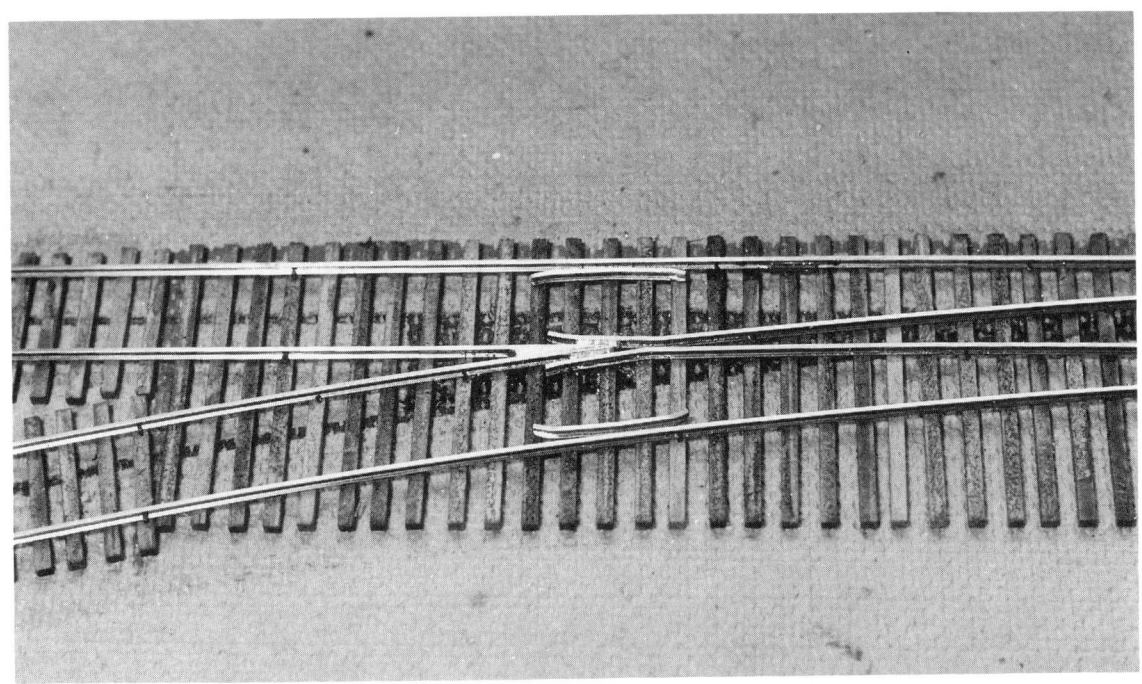

Fig. 3-17. Guard rails are added at frog section.

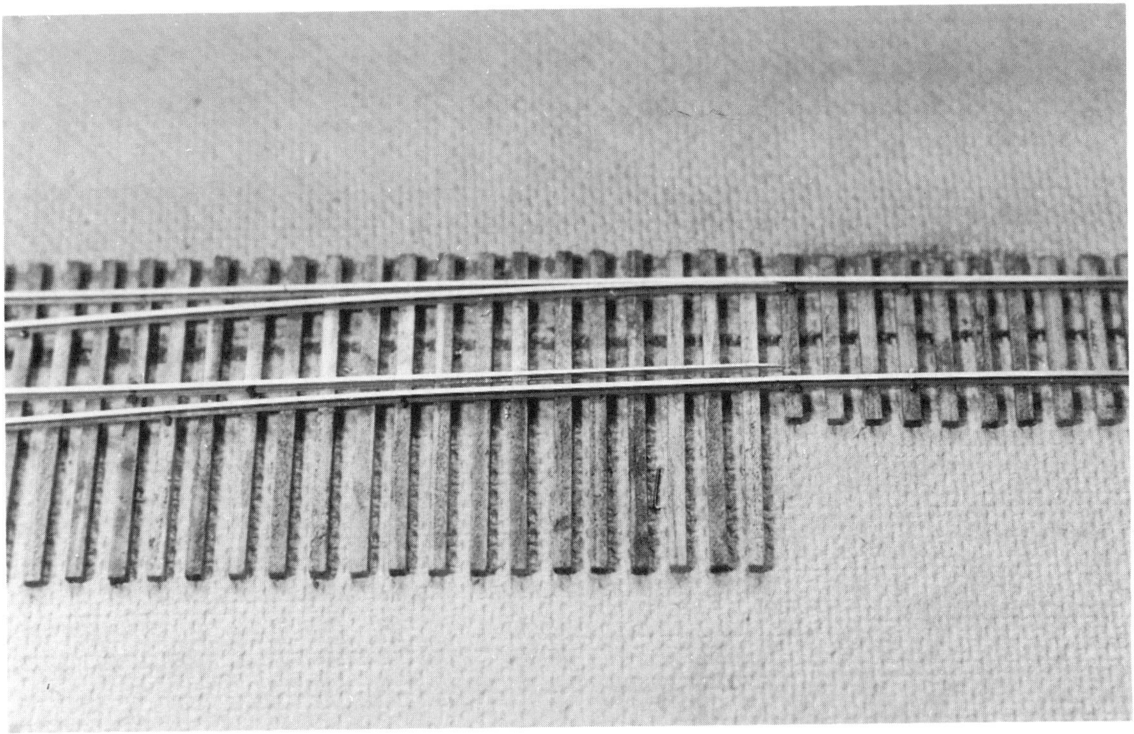

Fig. 3-18. Points are filed, and check prior to adding cross bar.

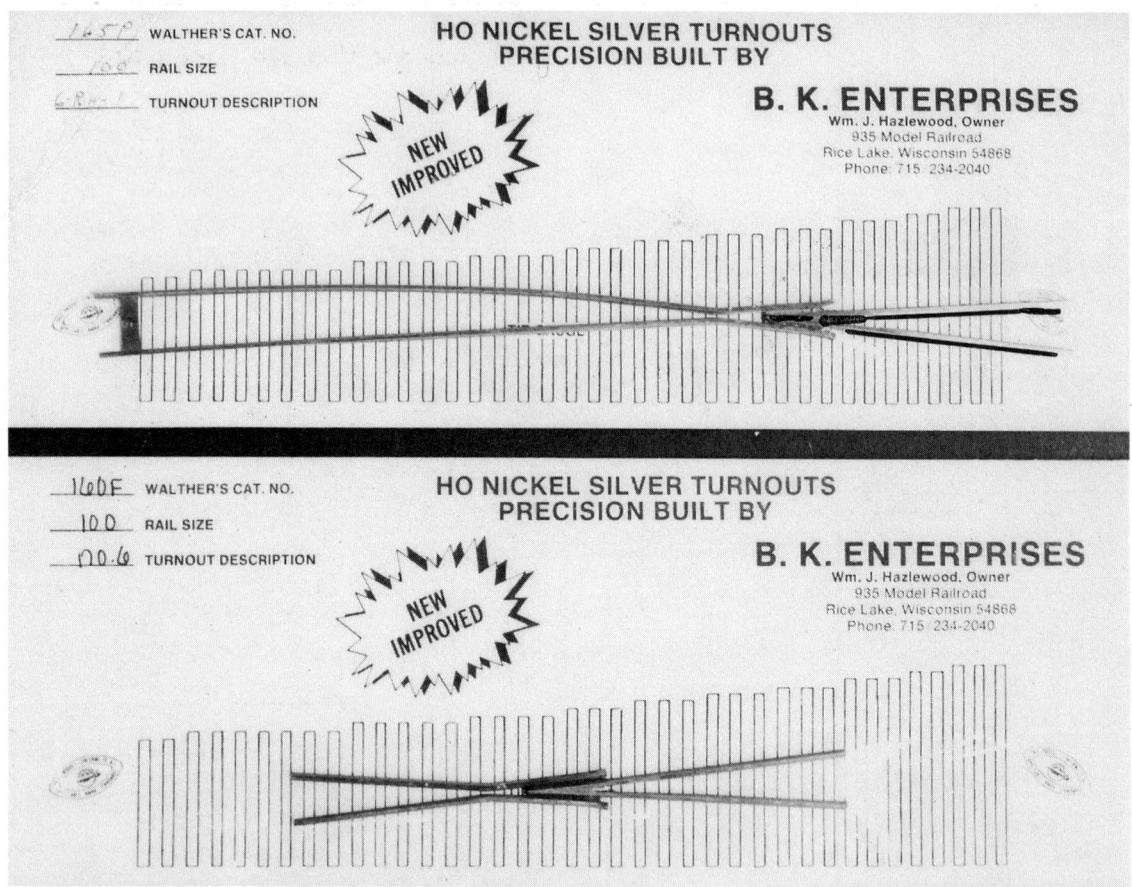

_165P_ WALTHER'S CAT. NO.
_100_ RAIL SIZE
_6RH-1_ TURNOUT DESCRIPTION

**HO NICKEL SILVER TURNOUTS
PRECISION BUILT BY**

B. K. ENTERPRISES
Wm. J. Hazlewood, Owner
935 Model Railroad
Rice Lake, Wisconsin 54868
Phone: 715 234-2040

NEW IMPROVED

_160F_ WALTHER'S CAT. NO.
_100_ RAIL SIZE
_no.6_ TURNOUT DESCRIPTION

**HO NICKEL SILVER TURNOUTS
PRECISION BUILT BY**

B. K. ENTERPRISES
Wm. J. Hazlewood, Owner
935 Model Railroad
Rice Lake, Wisconsin 54868
Phone: 715 234-2040

NEW IMPROVED

Fig. 3-19. For the scratchbuilt look with the least headaches: magnificent B.K. Enterprises pre-fabbed frogs, and pre-fabbed frog and point sections.

using the frog as the center guide. After the frog (or frog and point) section is secured, the stock rails are gauged and spiked into place. B. K. also markets a line of turnouts completely assembled save for ties. The pre-fabbed turnouts are spiked down, and after they are aligned and secured, the three metal gauge straps for pre-gauging the turnout components are removed and you have a realistic turnout equal in quality to a completely handmade unit.

SWITCH MACHINES

To properly activate and manipulate (throw) the turnouts you must install switch machines, which are basically sophisticated solenoids. There are a number of switch machines marketed, as can be seen when perusing the Walthers catalog.

For availability and all around dependability, my preference is the New Jersey International machine that can be surface mounted or under-the-layout mounted. Ideal mounting is the under-the-layout route, though more work is involved because a special linkage must be constructed to allow the hidden unit to activate the switch. If the less desirable but easily functional surface table mounting procedure is selected, a small shed or trackside structure should be built over the machine to conceal it. Prominent, visible switch mechanisms only detract from the layout's appearance.

The two alternate switch machine mounting possibilities are illustrated in Fig. 3-20. Diagrams

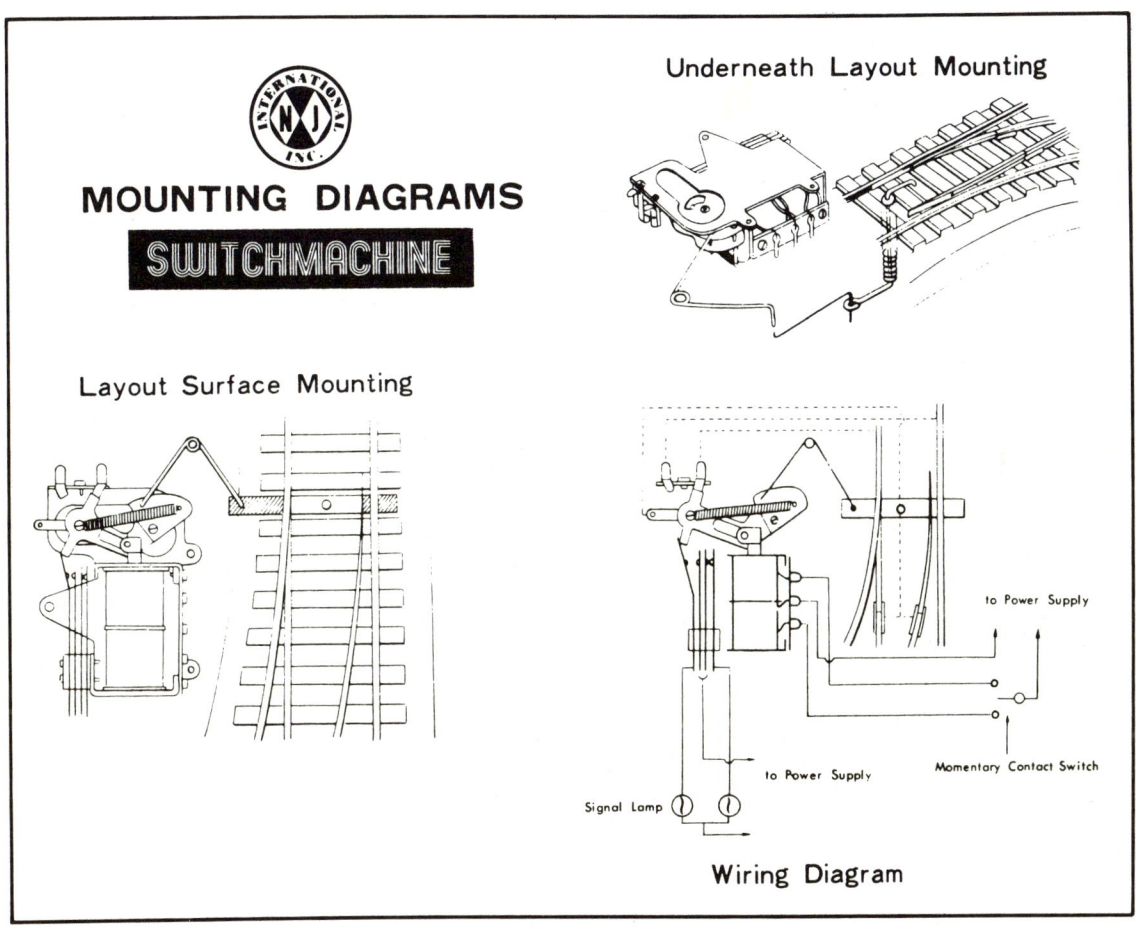

MOUNTING DIAGRAMS

SWITCHMACHINE

Layout Surface Mounting

Underneath Layout Mounting

to Power Supply

Momentary Contact Switch

to Power Supply

Signal Lamp

Wiring Diagram

Fig. 3-20. Typical switch installations. (Courtesy N.J. International)

show proper placement of the New Jersey International Switchmachine.

Another interesting switch machine concept is the one promoted by Railway Engineering called the Rotor-Motor. The Rotor-Motor uses a linked rotary action to move the switch points back and forth. As opposed to the snap-back-and-forth action of solenoid machines, the rotary action allows the points to slide quietly back and forth in a smooth action similar to prototype turnout movement.

Whatever trackwork alternates are chosen, study prototype situations and try to duplicate and emulate them wherever possible. Trackwork can be an important scenic and visual additive if properly constructed and detailed.

Chapter 4

Trees and Shrubbery

Trees and shrubs are the "icing on the cake" in scenic effects. With shrubbery and greenery added, color and extra dimension are introduced. At one time virtually all trees had to be scratch-built since only a few types of store-bought items were available. Today, even store-bought trees can be quite sophisticated, with enough modeling leeway built in to allow individualization liberties for each and every modeler.

Some store-bought trees leave a lot to be desired. I will present what I feel to be the best, most vivid and realistic tree packages available. I will also include some scratchbuilding alternatives I feel are effective, and within the scratchbuilding realms of the neophyte.

BUSHES

The old standby for bushes is Norwegian lichen, a very realistic-looking material that simulates small bushes in its natural state. Lichen is dyed various colors and packaged in boxes. For more authentic-looking shrubbery, one should stay away from the bright green packaged lichen. It appears garish and overstated when applied on a layout. Instead, select the duller greens and, if possible, obtain the multicolor lichen package assortments. Natural foliage is never monochromatic overall; model foliage should be no different.

Lichen can be glued down sporadically over the layout: in flat areas, on hills, rocks, etc. Some lichen pieces are long and make attractive tall bushes, but are unable to stand on end by themselves. In such cases, just place the piece over a finishing nail of the correct height driven a little way into the tabletop and slip the bush over the nail, which serves to support the long lichen clump.

For extra-small shrubbery and bushes, colored sponge is most effective—the household type available at supermarket and hardware stores. To make this shrubbery medium in quantity, tear sponge into 1-inch pieces and throw them into a blender. This processes the sponge nicely, giving you an assortment of vegetation pieces that work into the layout. Ballast cement or Elmers glue thinned one-to-one with water makes an excellent adhesive for this homemade sponge turf.

Railroad supply shops usually carry a full assortment of Woodland Scenics turf in various colors. In many instances it is superior appearance-wise to the homemade, since the turfs are specifically formulated to simulate ground cover.

Lichen is also effective for producing trees. It was an old standby in the early model railroading days when the denser lichen pieces were interworked into handmade trunk frameworks. Woodland Scenics tree foliage (available in their tree kits or packaged separately) is comparatively more effective, easier to use, and natural in appearance.

Sawdust Bushes

Our old, cheap, easily obtained buddy—sawdust—can be efficiently used to form simple bushes. Used properly, sawdust can be manipulated to simulate realistic bulk ground covering.

To make a working solution, take a cupful of sawdust and to it add a solution of white glue (one part glue, one part water) and mix. Add enough glue solution to the sawdust to make a heavy, paste-like, moldable solution. Then add some coloring (depending on the color saturation or hue desired). Water-based colors are the only toning types applicable.

Spoon the precolored, working solution onto the layout in areas where bushy ground cover is desired. Make miniature bush formations by pressing down the applied sawdust media. High bushes can be produced by spooning on the sawdust in thick, heavy dabs or clusters. Allow the sawdust-glue medium to dry to a workable consistency, then texture and sculpt the bushes with an X-acto knife containing a No. 11 blade. Breaking up and modeling the sawdust clumps will add a realistic appearance.

IVY AND CLIMBING VEGETATION

Ivy and vinework are easily simulated and can do much to enhance a building facade. They add to wall texture while introducing additive coloration. They can be used heavily or sporadically, allowing the stonework to show through and harmonize with the decorative additive foliage. Ivy can range in saturation and covering from a few inches in width or depth to patches over a foot. In reproductive modeling we can recreate thin vegetation effects or heavy three-dimensional saturated covering effects.

The first step in recreating ivy is laying out the vines. To simulate vines, I prefer heavy green sewing thread that can be used singly to simulate runners, or in disorganized, cluttered sections. Study real ivy and you will see the natural tendencies of this climbing vegetation. the thread or "vinework" can be attached with super glue. It should be tacked at various points and allowed to hang away from the wall at other points. In clumps along the vinework, in varied density, foliage is added using sawdust or Woodland Scenics light turf.

TREES

Trees are one of the mainstays of scenic effects. They are simple to reproduce in small scale and readily available in many types and kits for modelers who prefer the pre-fabbed approach to tree construction.

Tree kits can be found in abundance in the Walthers catalog and are manufactured by Woodland Scenics, Campbell Scale Models, Robert Brinkworth (who has an outstanding selection of handmade trees), Scenic Craft, and Treelines Co., sources whose mailing addresses can be found in the Appendix.

Woodland Scenics, one of the leaders in kit trees, has a construction concept that is novel and most effective. The Woodland Scenics kits contain bendable metal trunk castings with bark lines and textures. The trunks and limbs can be bent to any configuration. No two trees need to be the same.

Trunks, after they are bent to the desired shape, are painted using tube acrylics or Floquil matte lacquers. The trunks may also be brush detailed prior to foliage placement. The foliage material is then torn and separated into small (about 1- to 1 1/2-inch segments) and placed and glued on the limbs. With such versatile design and construction aspects trees can vary in design, shape, and foliage density with results as limitless as one's imagination. These trunk and foliage kits (Fig. 4-1)

are available in various boxed versions: forked trunk, straight trunk, shag bark, double fork, gnarled, shade tree, softwood pine, forest hardwood, forest pine.

Readers interested in the Woodland Scenics concept can send for their excellent catalog and reference manual in color, which features many ideas and approaches to creative tree and shrubbery fabrication.

Another fine kit, my favorite for full, lush tree structuring is Walthers "Gnarled Oaks" kit as shown in photo on page 47 and Fig. 4-2. This magnificent kit offers enough material to construct three very formidable oak trees. The trunks are of wood material (taken from natural sources), making them exceedingly realistic. The foliage material provided is the best kind available and trees from this kit duplicate real oaks in exacting detail, as seen in the photo on page 47. This tree can also be studied in the color section of this book.

Pine Trees

The pine tree is as awesome in real life as it is in model form. There are a number of avenues we can traverse with this gender of tree, from simple pine to the huge Western Ponderosa type that always appear grandiose in model pike situations.

Woodland Scenics with their cast metal trunk concept offers a number of pine tree kits. Walthers offers a few similar ones, but with detailed molded plastic trunkwork that can be most convincing when properly painted and detailed with scale model flat enamels, tubed acrylics, or Floquil lacquers. The pine tree kits compiled contain enough material to design and fabricate five 6-to-9-inch massive pines. Large-quantity kits that are more economical can also be purchased, containing adequate material to make 24 pine trees ranging in height from 2 to 4 inches.

Air Fern is another old but effective means of simulating pine trees. Air Fern can be found in the better model railroad supply hobby shops. It is a natural material treated with preservatives and stained to make it resilient and attractive.

Color Rite Scenery Products offers an excellent pine tree kit that utilizes Air Fern as the prime

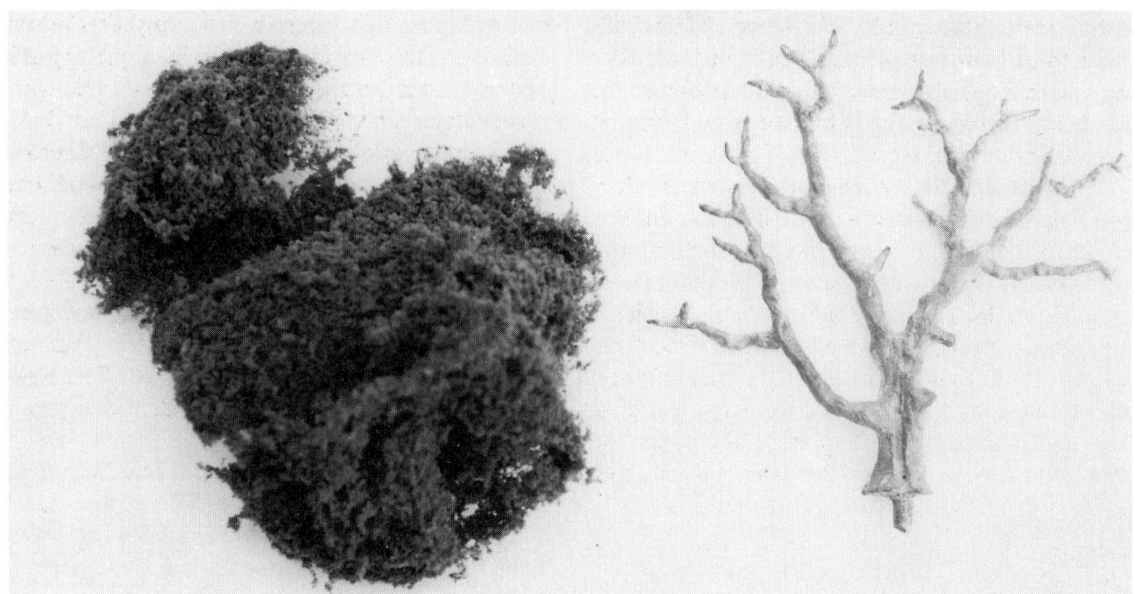

Fig. 4-1. The Woodland Scenics hardwood trees feature attractive foliage and a bendable soft metal detailed trunk.

Fig. 4-2. Walthers ''Gnarled Oaks,'' realism supreme.

foliage material (Fig. 4-3). The trunk material for these trees is of a tough but flexible plastic that must be painted for improved trunk appearance. Three kits are marketed; a 60-foot, a 40-foot, and a combination of the two sizes. Two trunk types are available: one for flat mounting, and one for hillside mounting in which the trunk bases are angled.

A special tool to be used in conjunction with a pin vise is also provided that serves to both puncture the trunks and insert the Air Fern. The tool is inserted into a pin vise. It is a miniature steel awl with a hole in the forward section, similar to the eye of a needle, that is pushed through the trunk. A piece of Air Fern (thick end portion) is inserted about 1/2 inch into the elongated opening of the special awl (Fig. 4-4). Then the awl tip pulls the Air Fern piece through the punched hole, placing the end out about 1 inch. The procedure is continued up and down the trunk while the trunk is revolved about an eighth of a turn prior to punching the consecutive hole (Fig. 4-5). The excess fern should not be cut as it is pulled through, but left to serve as a dead or sparse branch on the opposite side.

Each consecutive branch should be placed about 3/16 inch above or below the previously inserted limbs. Staggering the consecutive layers of branches makes for a more natural look. The lowest branch on the trunk should be at least 1 3/4 inches from the base.

All fern pieces supplied are extra long, and

Fig. 4-3. The Air Fern tree kit features fern foliage and trunks to make distinctive pine trees.

Fig. 4-4. The special tool is utilized to pierce the trunk and pull through the Air Fern.

Fig. 4-5. Building up the foliage.

Fig. 4-6. Finished Air Fern pine.

wire entwined and soldered together. Tape (1/8-inch masking) is wrapped around the trunk (as shown on the lower portion) to conceal the wire and add body. Then the completed trunk is painted and foliage is added as prescribed in the previous kit approaches.

Fig. 4-7. How a trunk armature is built up.

trimming is advised in order to give the tree a balanced look. Figure 4-6 shows a completed Air Fern pine very authentic in appearance. If you wish to add fullness to the existing finished tree, spray it with spray adhesive and roll it in Woodland Scenics coarse turf material.

Trees From Scratch

Building trees from scratch is the ultimate way to go, as well as the most economical. For full trees such as oaks, shade trees, and hardwoods, trunks can be made from wire, rod, and tubing. Figure 4-7 shows a favored approach to trunk construction. The heavy, thick section is of 1/8-to-3/16-inch brass tubing. The branches are of heavy brass rod and

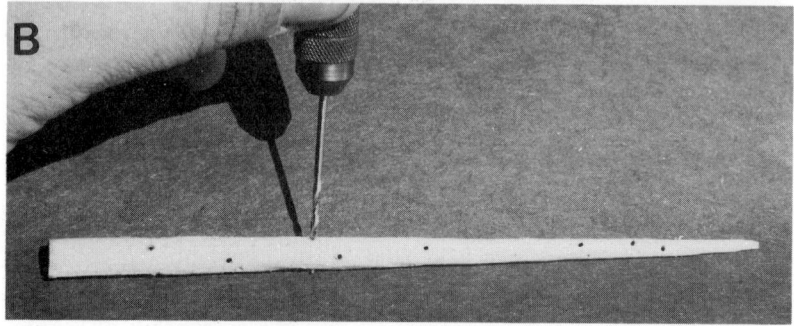

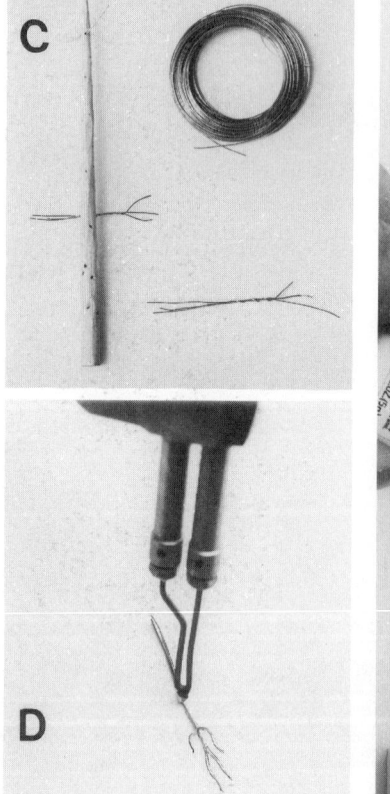

Fig. 4-8. Composite showing how a pine tree is constructed (see text for detailing).

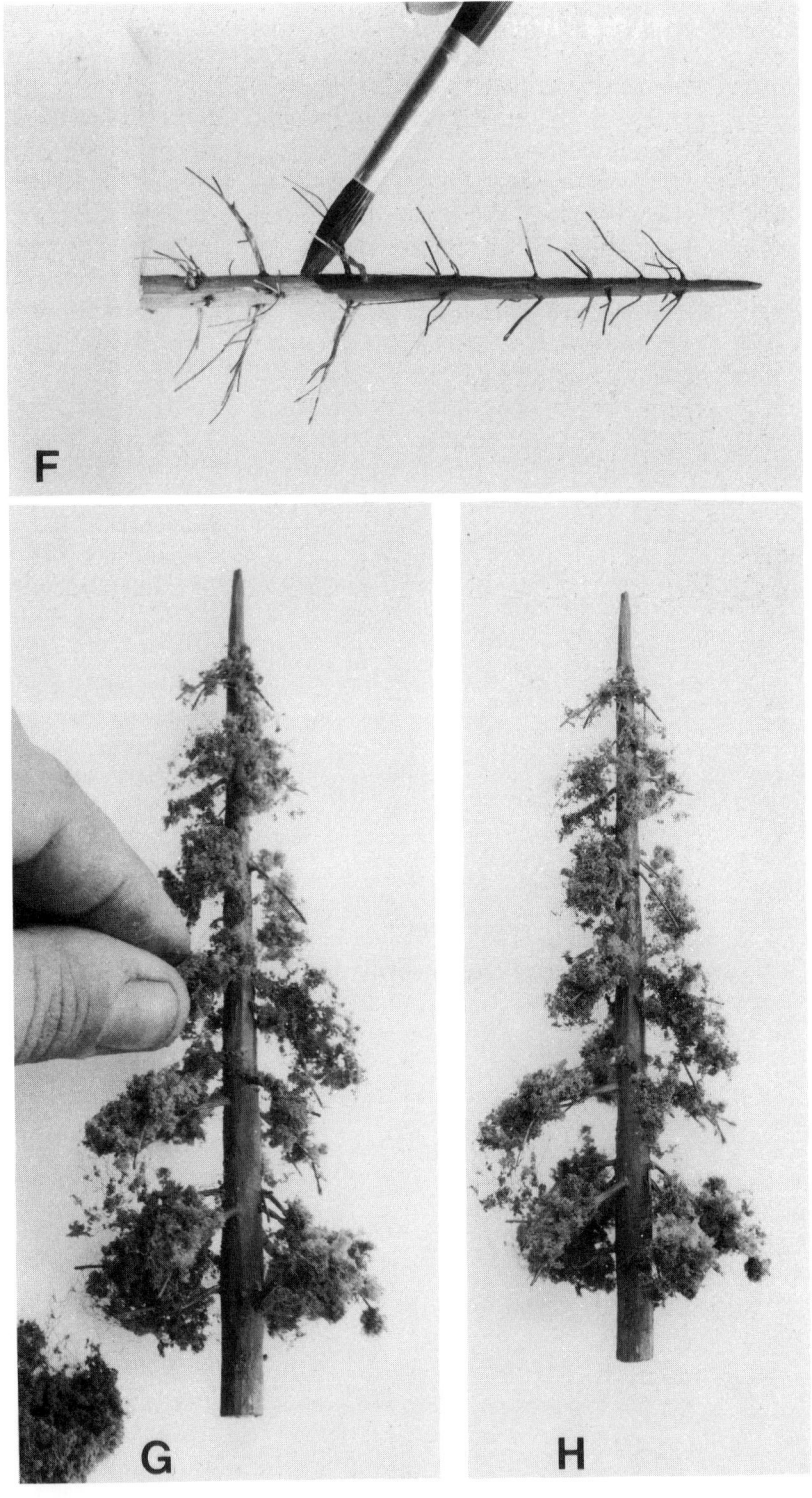

F

G

H

Fig. 4-9. Sans foliage the pine skeleton makes an authentic dead tree.

My particular approach to pine trees is featured next, step by step. I advocate realism to the greatest degree and this method gives me the best-looking pine tree. Hardware store dowels serve as the ba-

sis for the trunk: 1/2- and 1/8-inch widths are the only two utilized thicknesses. Length depends on the size tree to be modeled. The dowel is irregularly shaped and carved by hand as in Fig. 4-8 (A). Holes are then drilled at various points around the trunk with irregular spacing (B). A 1/64-inch drill bit in a pin vise serves this purpose. Limbs are constructed using fine copper wire (C) twisted together and allowed to spread irregularly at the ends. To add thickness to the branches, they are soldered (D). Enough solder is used so that it will flow along the branch and build up thickness. The branches are then inserted into the pre-drilled holes and secured (E) with super glue. The framework is painted with tubed acrylic paint (F). Woodland Scenics foliage material is pressed onto the branches (G) and secured with super glue. The foliage is saturated thoroughly with the super glue to make the foliage permanent while also adding body and strength.

The finished tree (H) is realistic, attractive, and by no means fragile. This same tree can be seen in the color plate section properly placed in a scenic surrounding it was designed for.

You can also model this pine in a dead tree version. The trunk and limbs are painted and left sans foliage (Fig. 4-9).

Trees are simple to put together whether scratch or store-bought. They do much to enhance scenic locales used singly or in groups. Any attempt at tree fabrication will prove fruitful regardless of whether they are built by beginning or advanced modelers.

Chapter 5

Modeling Water

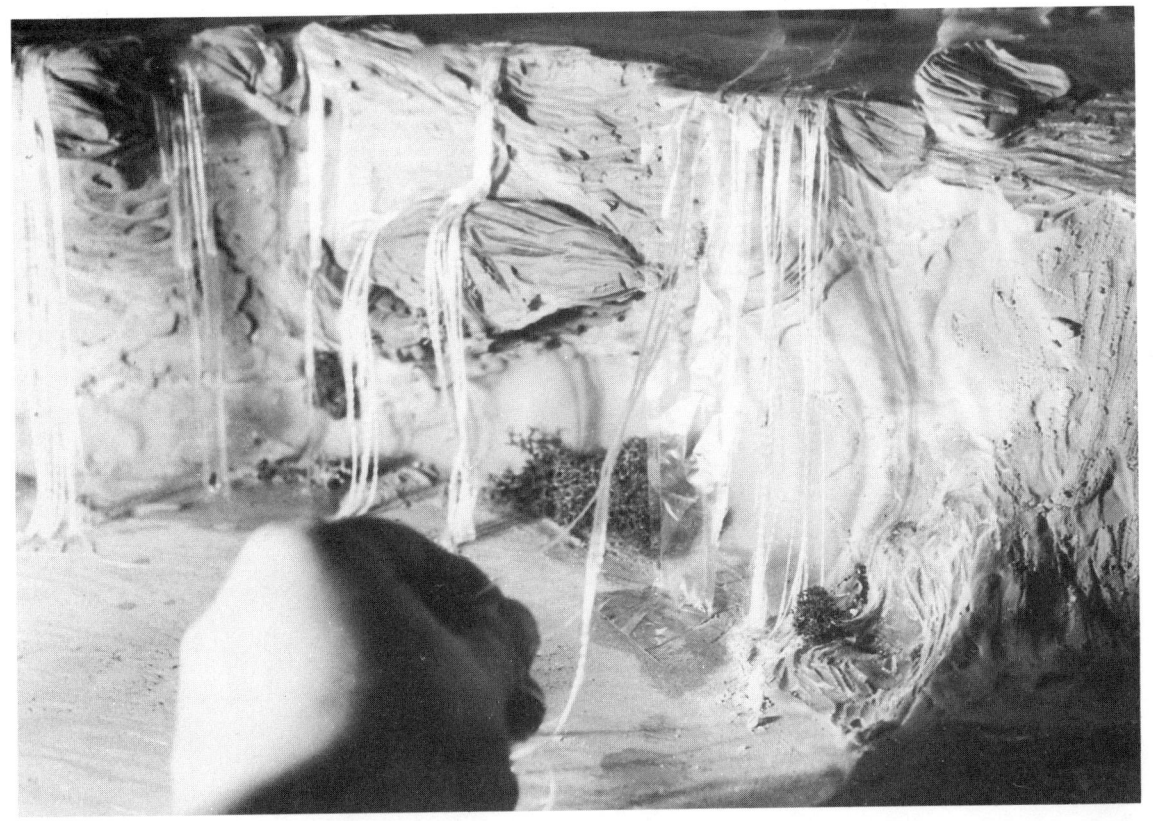

ater and waterways add a touch of life to the model pike. Water can be easy or difficult to model, depending on what types you wish to duplicate. Running or turbulent water must be more exactingly modeled or it will not look real. The techniques chosen here are kept basic and not too involved; good starting-off projects that anyone can undertake with pleasing results.

PLASTER AND VARNISH

This is the oldest method, inaugurated before liquid casting plastic existed. Water was modeled using poured plaster that was allowed to semi-harden, after which waves and rivulets were worked in with the fingers or modeling tools. After the shaping and modeling, the plaster hardened and was painted.

Topcoating with four or five coats of varnish or clear enamel gave the plaster facsimile its wet look. This is a compromise approach and not too popular anymore. Some interesting results can be obtained with this method, but it is not as striking or as authentic-looking as the others described here.

A DIMENSIONAL LAKE

This technique is best used for producing deep, large bodies of water (big ponds, lakes, etc.). Liquid casting plastic may also be used in such situations, but you would need to use a great amount of it, which would up the expense. An alternative is to model and detail the waterbed, which is recessed, and top it with a sheet of clear 1/8-inch Lucite for the lake's surface.

Fig. 5-1. The waterbed is modeled after cutting an approximate opening in the tabletop.

For starters, cut an opening into the tabletop the desired shape of the body of water. A wire screen "basket" serves as the waterbed framework. Lay plaster-soaked newspaper around the waterbed base. (The plaster-paper-framework technique was explained in Chapter 2.) While the plaster is still wet, smooth and model the bed (Fig. 5-1).

When the waterbed is dry, paint it with Latex paint. Color choice is optional; one person might prefer a dark waterbed base, another a sandy light base. The color should, however, match the tonality and hue of the surrounding embankments and ground area (Fig. 5-2). Now add the finish textures and details. Put the earth, rock, and vegetation (Fig. 5-3) into place. You can scatter a few twigs about to duplicate submerged logs.

Next, cut the 1/8-inch-thick Lucite sheeting to size. Lucite can be cut on a bandsaw or by hand with the aid of a jewelers or fine compass saw. Place the Lucite sheet over the recessed water bed and screw down into place (Fig. 5-4). For added realism and to heighten the depth effect, the bottom of the Lucite sheet should be airbrushed with green acrylic lacquer toner (available at autobody paint shops), darker toward the central portion of the sheet. Build up the banks of the lake, following the contours of the constructed bed opening. Plaster of paris again serves this purpose.

Figure 5-5 shows the completed lake with completed banks and scenery. Note the depth and realism achieved with this technique. In Fig. 5-6 we see the brook feeding the lake, which is shallow and modeled using liquid casting plastic, a method covered in this chapter.

LIQUID CASTING PLASTIC

This is the most effective water modeling medium to date: It is easy to use and gives the most realistic results. Flowing water and depth effects are easy to realize with this revolutionary medium, originally introduced to give plastic coats to wood surfaces and decoupage pieces.

A number of liquid casting plastic products are marketed. All of these are resin based and contain two solutions: a resin and a hardener (catalyst) that must be intermixed in order to make a working so-

Fig. 5-2. The bed is now painted.

Fig. 5-3. Detailing and bed texturing is added.

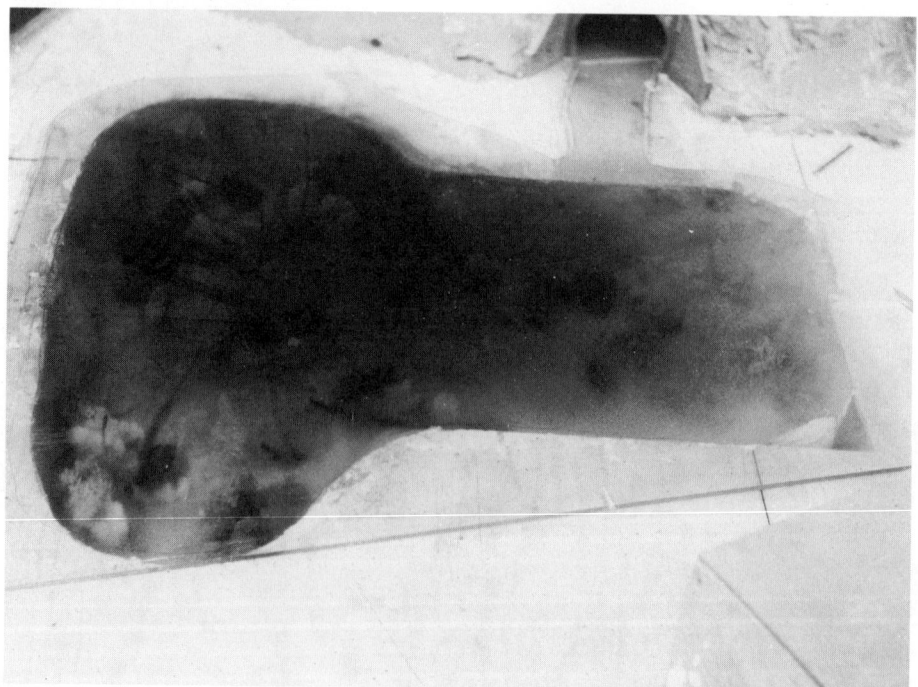

Fig. 5-4. A pre-painted Lucite sheet to serve as the lake's surface is put into place.

Fig. 5-5. The completed lake after the banks and outlying terrain are modeled.

Fig. 5-6. The brook tributary is shallow, so it can be simulated with poured casting plastic.

lution. Castolite and Enviro-Tex are the two fa-vored brands; for model railroading purposes Enviro-Tex seems to be the best. The two can be utilized for different situations: the Enviro-Tex when dry exhibits a smooth, flawless, even surface, whereas the Castolite dries to a rippled surface. For calm bodies of water Enviro-Tex is best; for a more textured surface Castolite gets the nod. (Polyester resin is described further in the chapter.)

Enviro-Tex, used exclusively for the modeling effects illustrated here, is mixed one to one (one part resin, one part hardener). The two solutions should be vigorously and thoroughly mixed in a clean container and whipped like pancake batter. There should be no need for concern if bubbles appear during the mixing; it signifies that the mixing procedure is going well. Mixing should be complete after about three minutes of vigorous agitation.

As soon as the solution is fully mixed, the plas-tic can be poured. Pour the solution evenly; if bub-bles remain, work them out with a pin or sharp stick. Once the solution is poured and the bubbles worked out, it should be allowed to set and harden—a process that takes all of 72 hours. If cast-ing thicknesses over 1/2 inch, it is best to do it in stages, casting or pouring 1/2 inch at a time and allowing full cure time between coats. When model-ing water over 1 inch deep, the Lucite sheet method described previously is the more favorable method.

A typical pond casting situation involving the use of poured Enviro-Tex is illustrated in Figs. 5-7, 5-8, 5-9. The pond recession is no deeper than 3/4 inch, an ideal depth for plastic casting. The bed was first painted with an airbrush, followed by textur-ing with weed, rocks, sand, and miscellaneous fo-liage material. The plastic was then poured slowly and evenly, and allowed to settle into the pond's bed.

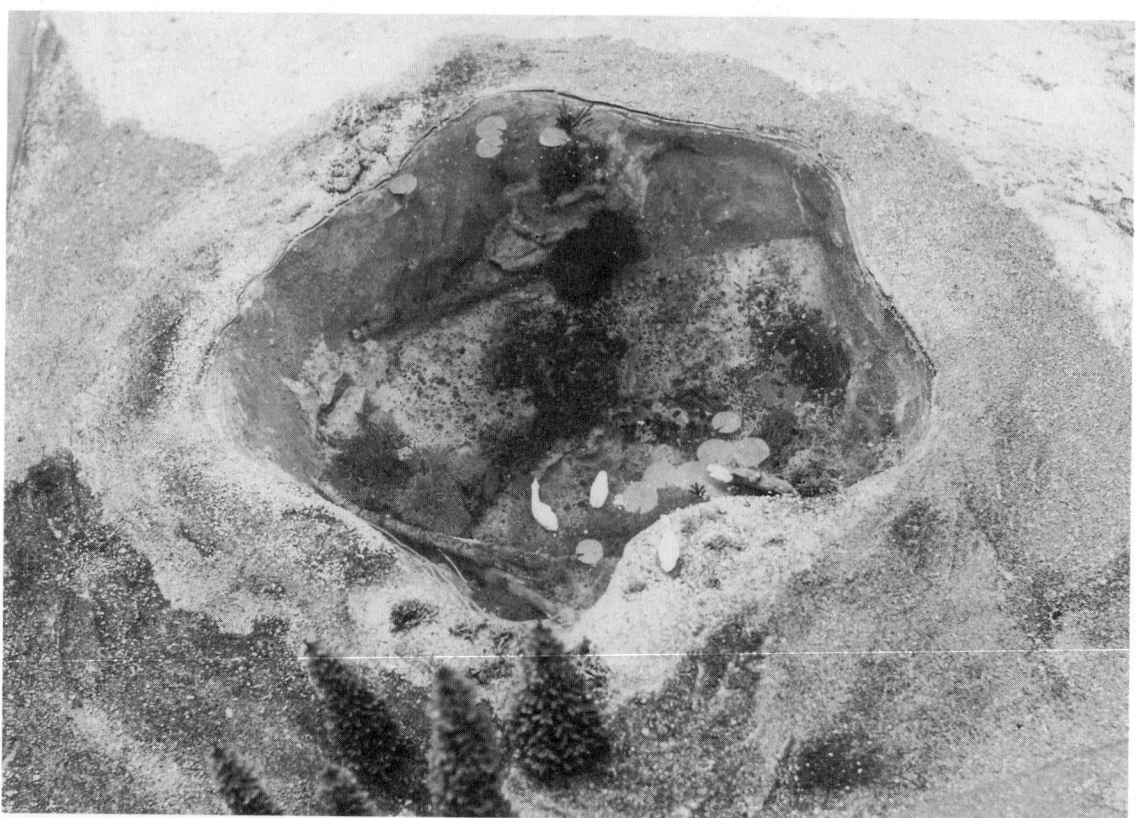

Fig. 5-7. A small 3-D pond complete with underwater modeling and swimming ducks.

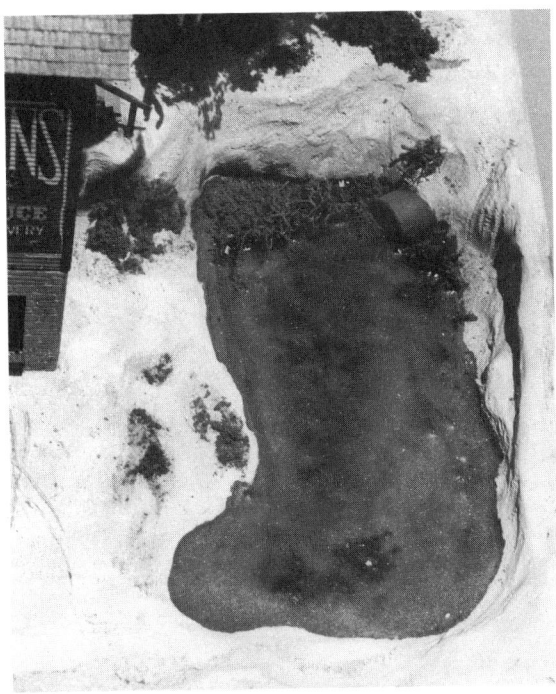

Fig. 5-8. Deeper cast plastic ponds should be built up in stages. After the first thickness has fully cured, the next layer is administered.

Before you pour, make certain that the piece to be filled is level or the finished water section will appear unnatural. If weeds, rocks, or half-submerged logs are to be added, now is the time—before the plastic solution begins to set. Casting plastic, no matter how carefully applied, tends to slightly crawl up the embankments on the peripheral edges of the body of water. This short-coming is inherent with casting plastic. The problem is not acute though; the creeping edges can be retouched and painted so that the edges appear natural. From initial pouring to hard setting, the casting plastic retains its wet look, making it the best choice for modeling water.

A QUIET WATERFALL

Waterfalls add life to the pike while giving the modeler excuses for introducing an occasional bridge here and there. The simple body of water modeled next I consider a "quiet" waterfall: not thunderous, spraying, or overwhelming. A body of

water of this nature can be handled easily by neo-phytes, particularly if they have progressed past the "pouring plastic" stage. White or torrential water-falls take a bit more expertise, time, and corrective and additive painting in order for them to appear realistic.

Here again we put into play our old water standby, casting plastic. We also implement the pouring technique, but with some additional modeling thrown in.

The pond constructed previously necessitated a simple base or recession in order to confine and retain the simulated water. For a waterfall, we must embark on a more sophisticated structuring approach: building the falling water framework. Because most waterfalls run over rocks, we must also model rockwork.

We first build a wood and screen wire framework as shown in Fig. 5-10. In-depth coverage on this type of framework construction was presented in Chapter 2. You will note in Fig. 5-10 that the upper 1/2-inch plywood framework piece is cut irregu-

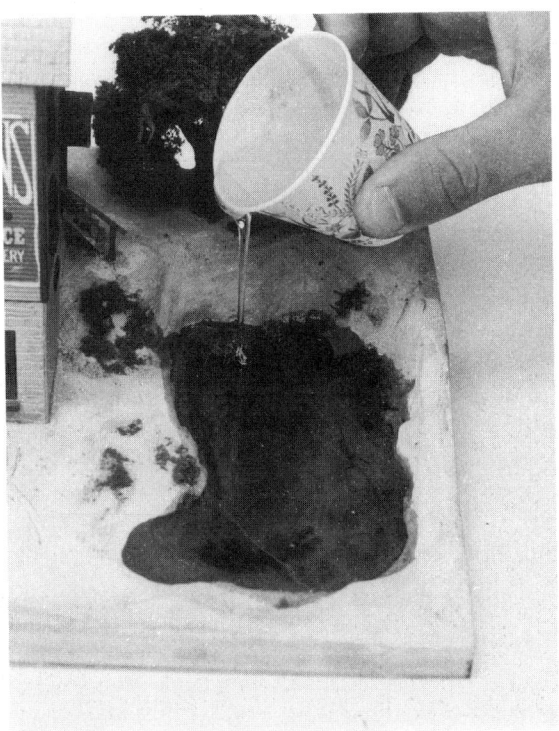

Fig. 5-9. Pour evenly, making sure the modeled piece is level.

Fig. 5-10. Building a wire screen and wood framework is the first step.

larly around the edges and recedes toward the middle. This will help make the finished waterfall appear to be flowing through a naturally eroded depression, as in actual situation. The screen framework is bent and contoured as desired.

A stiff solution of plaster of paris is mixed and applied to the screenwork. Areas simulating ground or dirt are smoothed over with the fingers prior to drying. Rockwork is modeled into the hardened plaster after it has set with the aid of a Dremel Tool (Fig. 5-11). Study real waterfalls both in nature and photographs to familiarize yourself with their proper evolution and structure. In areas where the rock would be worn smooth by the continuous passage of water, duplicate this effect by wearing away the rock with sandpaper as shown in Fig. 5-12. This will also form pockets to guide the flow and fall of the simulated water as the casting plastic is poured.

After all the modeling work is completed, the waterfall depression and all the peripheral areas are painted. The preferred painting method here is by airbrush or spraypainting (Fig. 5-13). Study Chapter 2 for hints and details on modeling rock and

groundwork. Waterfall-base modeling and painting is handled in the same manner as terrain and rock modeling. The only differing factor is the addition of simulated flowing water.

Now comes the tedious work: formulating the falling water. Because the casting plastic is liquid with no body of its own (until it sets) it must be poured over a foundation, preferably a semitransparent one. Pre-cut scotch tape is a good foundation medium, as is cellophane or wrapping plastic. Another excellent and sometimes preferred medium is spun fiberglass or "angel hair." Unfortunately this is not too readily available since it has been found to be harmful when improperly handled. An alternate solution is the use of fiberglass woven cloth obtainable at hardware stores.

Unravel and unweave this cloth until the strings that are used to drape over the rocks remain, as in the photo on page 57. The falling water should be routed to fall through appropriate places, namely the deepest and lowest recession points on the uppermost rocks (study photos). The waterfall constructed here features the fiberglass stringing, plus

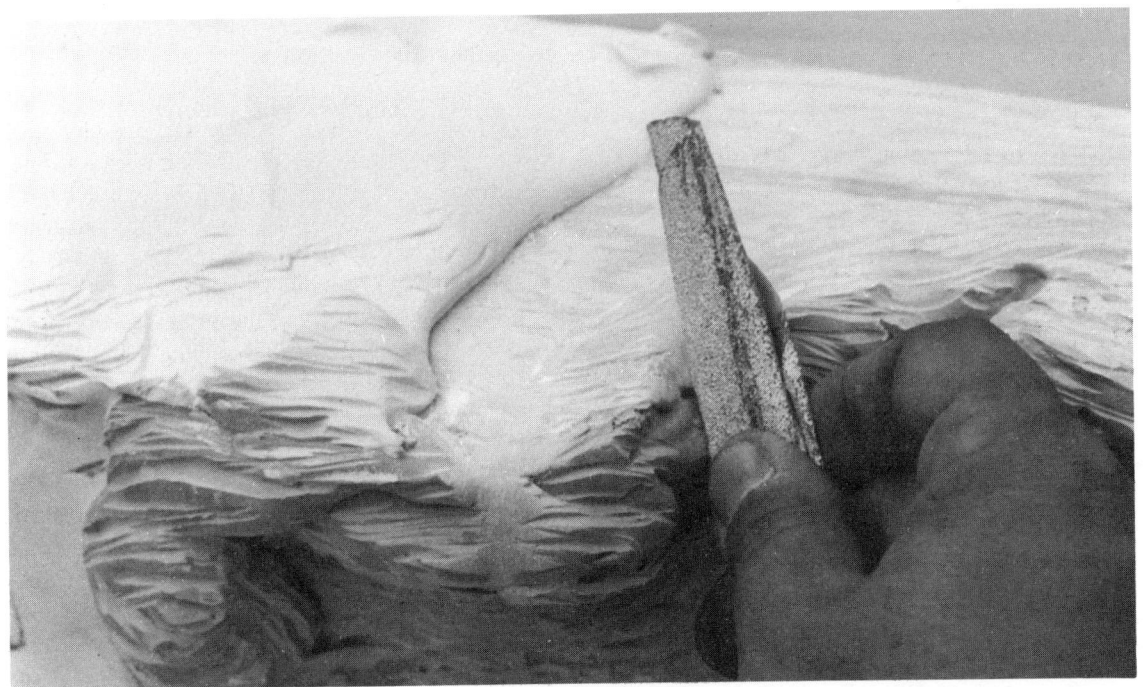

Fig. 5-11. Plaster serves as the modeling medium finish, detailed with a Dremel Tool and grinding wheel.

Fig. 5-12. Water-eroded rock bed segments are worked in with sandpaper.

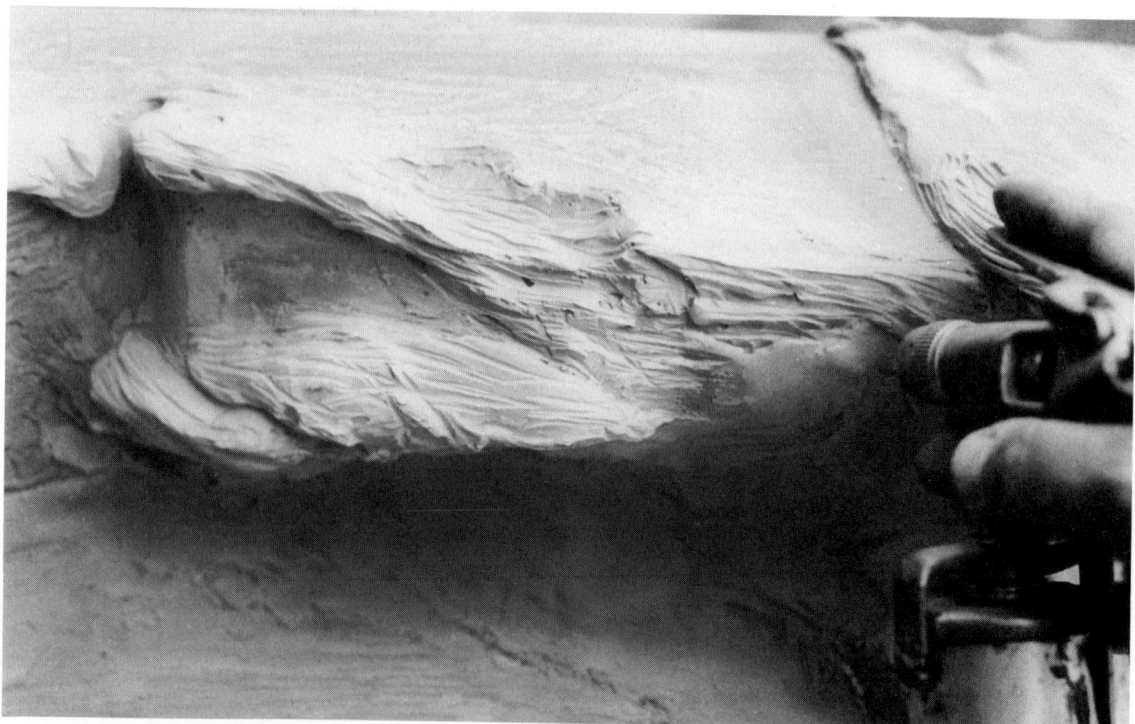

Fig. 5-13. Painting and shading takes place next. Here we utilized a Badger 400 detail gun, which is excellent for both small and large area work.

scotch tape, plus wrapping plastic to vary the falling water configurations.

After the water foundation material has been placed, pour the casting plastic. Pour slowly, allowing the plastic to work into the fibers and over the entire surfaces of the fibers (tape, cellophane, etc) as shown in Fig. 5-14. Pour at the top, allowing the plastic to run downward. After the running rivulets are coated, you can mix a larger volume of plastic to pour over the bed at the top of the waterfall and the recessed bed at the base of the waterfall.

This completes the construction aspects of the waterfall. Water can be highlighted and detailed using oil-based pigments for wave and spray effects. Figure 5-15 shows close-up details of the finished waterfall. The white spray and wavy effects where the falling water hits the body of water at the waterfall's base was produced with both airbrush and brush. Detailed photographs of this waterfall can

be further studied in the color section.

POLYESTER RESIN

Polyester resin is another pourable plastic medium not fully exploited in this chapter since it is not as easy or as convenient to use. Unlike the clear plastics mentioned before, true polyester resins exhibit a slight brown overall tone. The catalyst necessary to activate this solution is methyl ethyl ketone, a dangerous and toxic chemical that can be harmful to the skin and lungs, another reason polyester resin is not a favored medium. This solution is so strong that it can affect some plastics and paints by dissolving and softening them. The only pro factor with polyester resin is that it can be tinted using special dyes marketed for the product.

Refer to the Appendix for a listing of the specialized casting plastics described and their sources.

Fig. 5-14. Plastic is then poured slowly and evenly.

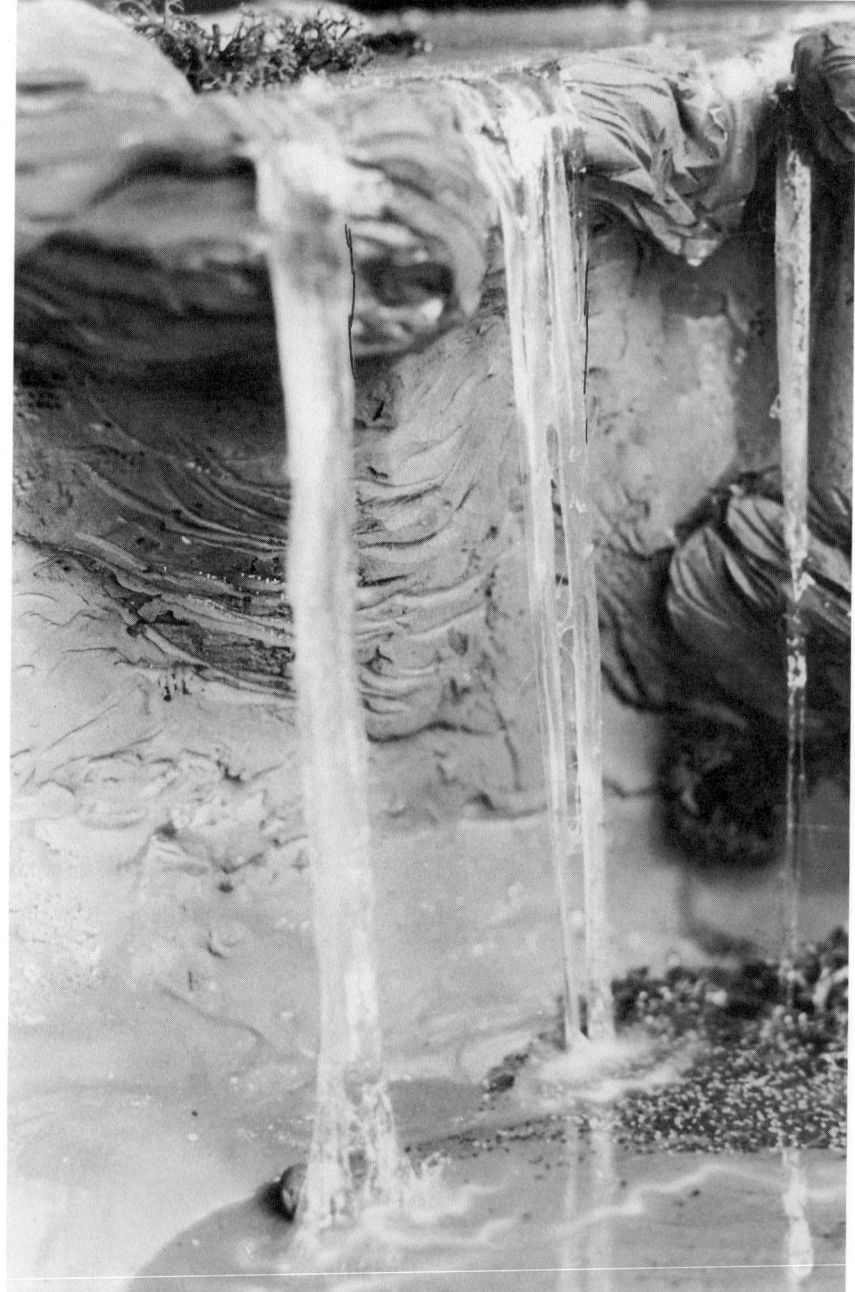

Fig. 5-15. Close up detail of a waterfall segment. Left hand water segment is fiberglass fiber saturated with plastic; center and right flows of water are scotch tape covered with plastic. Splashing, spray and waves at the base of each waterfall segment was simulated by airbrush and drybrush application.

Chapter 6

Bridging the Gaps

B ridgework is an integral aspect of the well-conceived model pike. Properly designed scenic terrain featuring mountains, valleys, and waterways should include some form of bridgework to span the spaces and add scenic and decorative touches. When adding bridges to the pike, you must consider the type of bridge that adequately suits the terrain. For example: you don't find a steel truss, or deck girder steel bridge, or poured concrete viaduct in the inaccessible wilderness. For rugged wilderness and high mountain locales, timber bridges are the way to go because these were the types that could be constructed using materials at hand, usually wood. Occasionally a stone bridge or viaduct would make an appearance (usually near a sizeable town) in the outer regions, again governed by the availability of stone and means to quarry it.

Railroad modelers and scratchbuilders are most fortunate since they have at their disposal unlimited scratchbuilding material and parts resources. For the more timid, basic modelers, a wealth of bridge kits of all types are available from many manufacturers, with fabrication relying on basic glueing or fastening together of a few structural parts. For the more serious builder, a great many craftsman-quality kits are marketed in wood, styrene, or other plastics. These kits go from simple to complex, depending on the types of structures involved.

WOODEN BRIDGES

By far the most classic, most attractive bridges (and sometimes the most complex in construction) are the wooden bridges—of which there are a few standard types. These include the Howe truss (Fig. 6-1), the covered (New England type, Fig. 6-2), and the timber deck bridges (Figs. 6-3 and 6-4). The other gap bridging structures that prevail are the trestles. Trestles can be small, basic, and simple (Fig. 6-5) or larger and more imposing (Figs. 6-6 and 6-7). These are the bridges common to timber country and outlying areas. In the photo on page 69, consummate artistry and craftsmanship is displayed in this highly detailed bridge structure on the Lauderdale Shore Line R.R. club layout. Model-work on this scratchbuilt structure entirely of wood

was executed by Bob Stewart.

The largest of the wooden bridges were the trestle types, attractive and enjoyably intricate to model and construct. Because wooden bridges were not as structurally sound as steel bridges, they should be used where they best apply—in pike situations not involving heavy locomotive equipment (articulateds, etc.).

Wooden bridges may be easily constructed using Northeastern basswood, but I would strongly recommend both laymen and purists to avail themselves of the fine wood bridge kits currently available through hobby shop outlets.

Campbell offers a host of bridges, all of which are pictured in this chapter. Of all the bridge structures marketed, they seem to be the best. Their prefab construction procedures and well-laid-out instruction sheets allow even the novice to tackle what seems a complex task with rewarding results.

S.S. Ltd. markets an interesting arch-type timber bridge called "Dinky Creek Bridge." It is attractive and very detailed, and may be obtained from Walthers. Most of the craftsman kits are well priced and easy to put together. You must, however, allow more time than usually allotted to a more simplified plastic type kit.

STONE BRIDGES

Stone bridges (concrete viaducts, etc.) are picturesque and fit into virtually all landscaping well. They can take the shape of solid full-face units (wall or dam), or they can be compositionally artistic (Fig. 6-8) and feature fancy archwork and relief concrete decor. Some excellent stone bridges and viaducts can be fabricated from scratch, but it involves intricate handwork, and in some cases a knowledge of casting techniques. Scratchbuilt (plaster) stonework and viaducts are best left to the master craftsman.

The most feasible solution for the builder interested in modeling stonework is the utilization of commercially cast stonework that can be decorated, detailed, and modified to suit. Most stone structure castings are unpainted and a little handbrush or airbrush work will turn them into small masterpieces, individualized by color and installation.

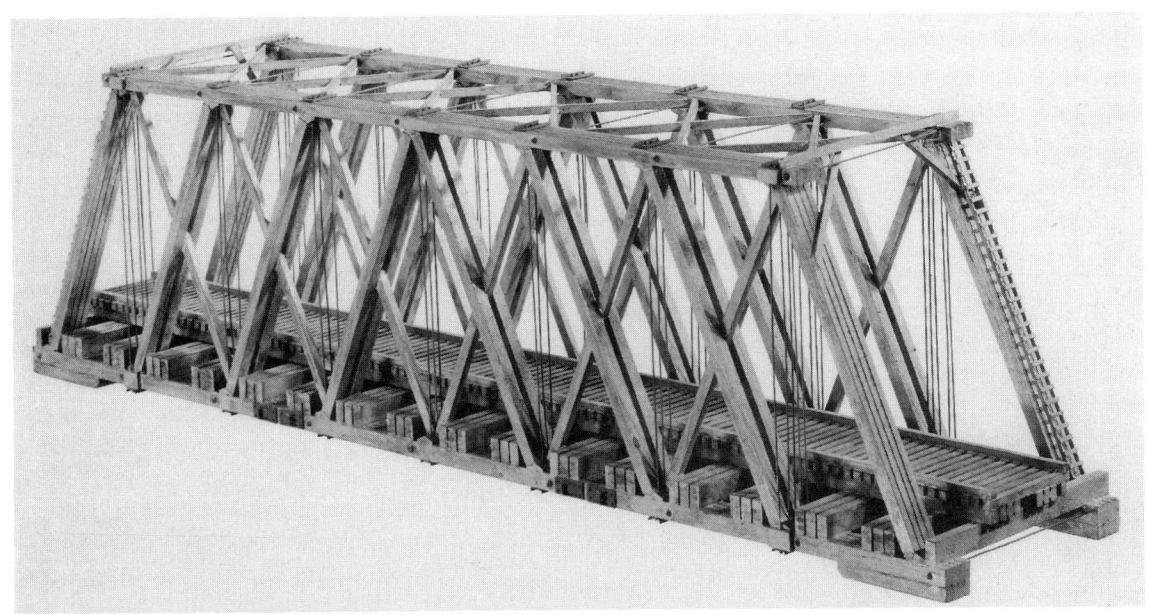

Fig. 6-1. The Howe wooden truss bridge. (Courtesy Campbell Scale Models)

Fig. 6-2. Covered bridge. (Courtesy Campbell Scale Models)

Fig. 6-3. A typical "Boonie" bridge; the Campbell deck timber bridge.

Fig. 6-4. Another backwoods classic: the Campbell Thru-Timber bridge.

Fig. 6-5. A simple open deck pile trestle. (Courtesy Campbell Scale Models)

Fig. 6-6. The straight timber trestle. (Courtesy Campbell Scale Models)

Fig. 6-7. For detailing and accuracy, the Campbell tall curved trestle reigns supreme. (Courtesy Campbell Scale Models)

Fig. 6-8. This magnificent stone bridge is another key scenic highlight on the Lauderdale Shore Line Model R.R. Club layout. Built from scratch from Hydrocal, it exhibits the fine craftsmanship of John Jetter.

The serious scratchbuilder might want to look into the various plastic sheeting materials that simulate a number of types of stonework. This plastic sheeting is excellent to work with, cuts easily with an X-acto knife, and gives most favorable and accurate results—particularly when painted and weathered properly. Holgate-Reynolds and S.S. Ltd. provide various types of stonework in sheet form, and they can be found in the Walthers catalog.

STEEL BRIDGES

Industrial locales usually sport a variety of steel bridges that enhance the overall sense of realism. Steel bridges can be small, such as plate girder and plate deck types, or larger and ornate, as the larger steel girder truss types. Here again, Campbell offers some superb pieces that are detailed to an infinite degree. Figure 6-9 shows the typical plate girder bridge and Fig. 6-10 displays a deck type

girder configuration. The larger truss type girder bridges, such as the single track and double track, are presented in Figs. 6-11 and 6-12.

The simplified plastic kit aficionado can find a number of steel bridges of all types and sizes available from Vollmer, Atlas, Faller, Heljan, Kibri, Josef, and Pola.

Scratchbuilding steel structured bridges can be a snap, particularly if one uses the Plastruct materials available at most hobby shops. Plastruct offers a variety of channel sizes, angles, girders, and various types and thicknesses of plastic sheeting. Bridge building with Plastruct shapes is quick and simple; the plastic is easy to cut with blade or zona saw and bonds together with styrene cement, epoxy, or super glue.

Starting with Fig. 6-13, you see a typical construction sequence of a truss bridge side, showing how simple and effective modern bridgework can be using Plastruct and simple model tooling.

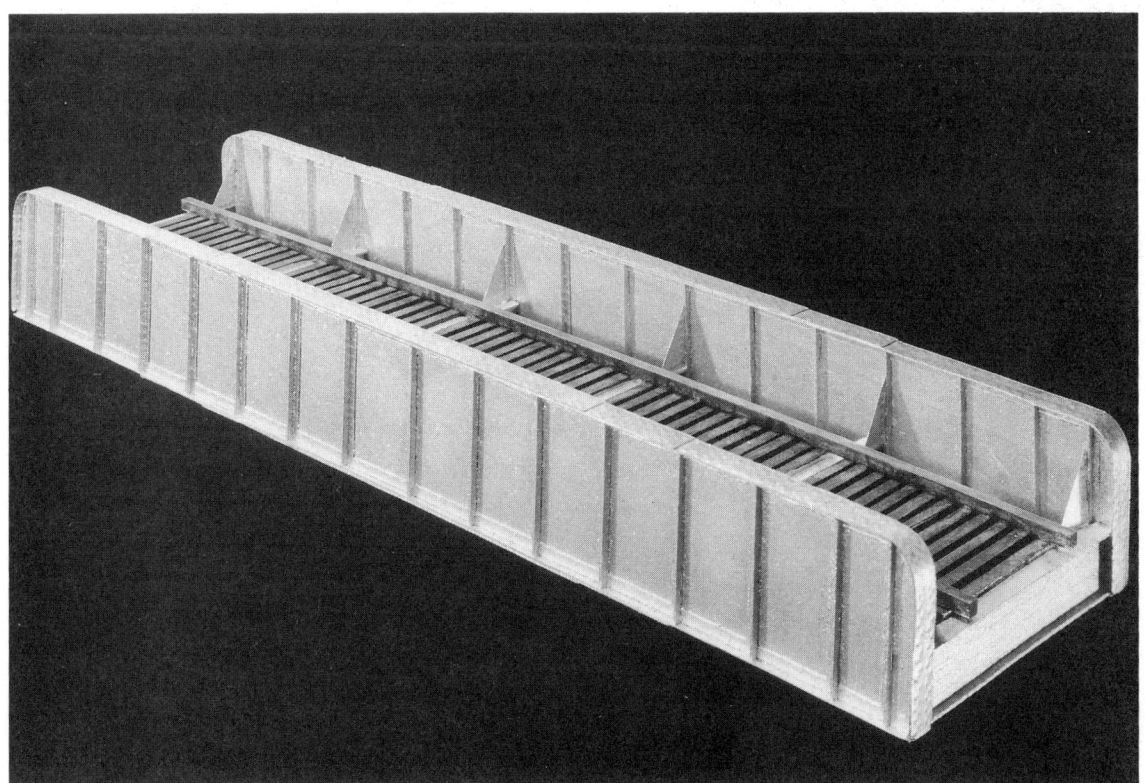

Fig. 6-9. Campbell's thru-plate girder bridge.

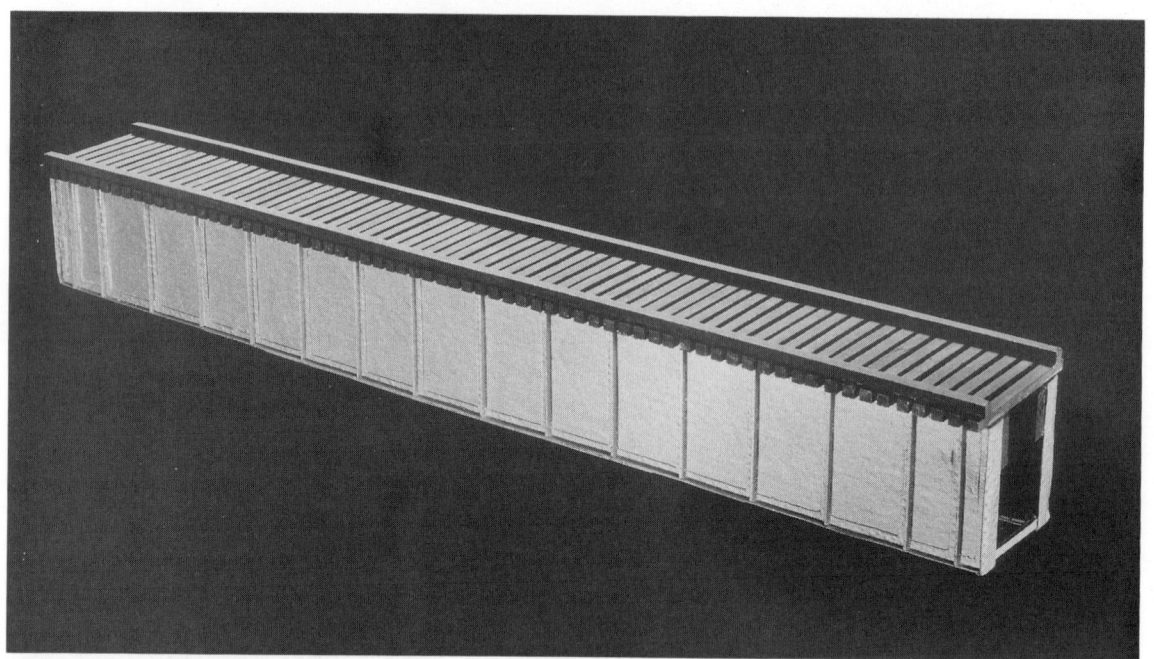

Fig. 6-10. Campbell's deck plate girder bridge.

Fig. 6-11. This double-track steel truss bridge by Campbell exhibits infinite detailing, adaptable to many layouts and situations. (Courtesy Campbell Scale Models)

Fig. 6-12. Another steel truss version by Campbell: a single-track truss. (Courtesy Campbell Scale Models)

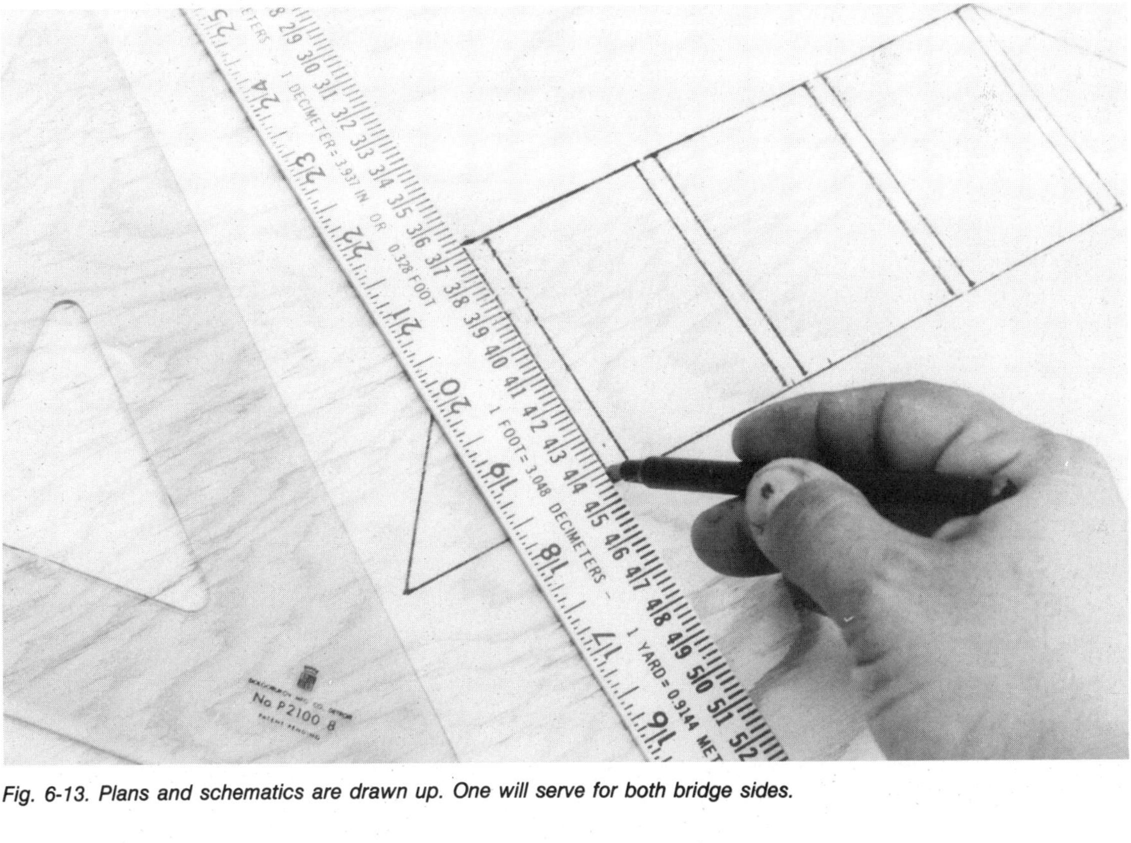

Fig. 6-13. Plans and schematics are drawn up. One will serve for both bridge sides.

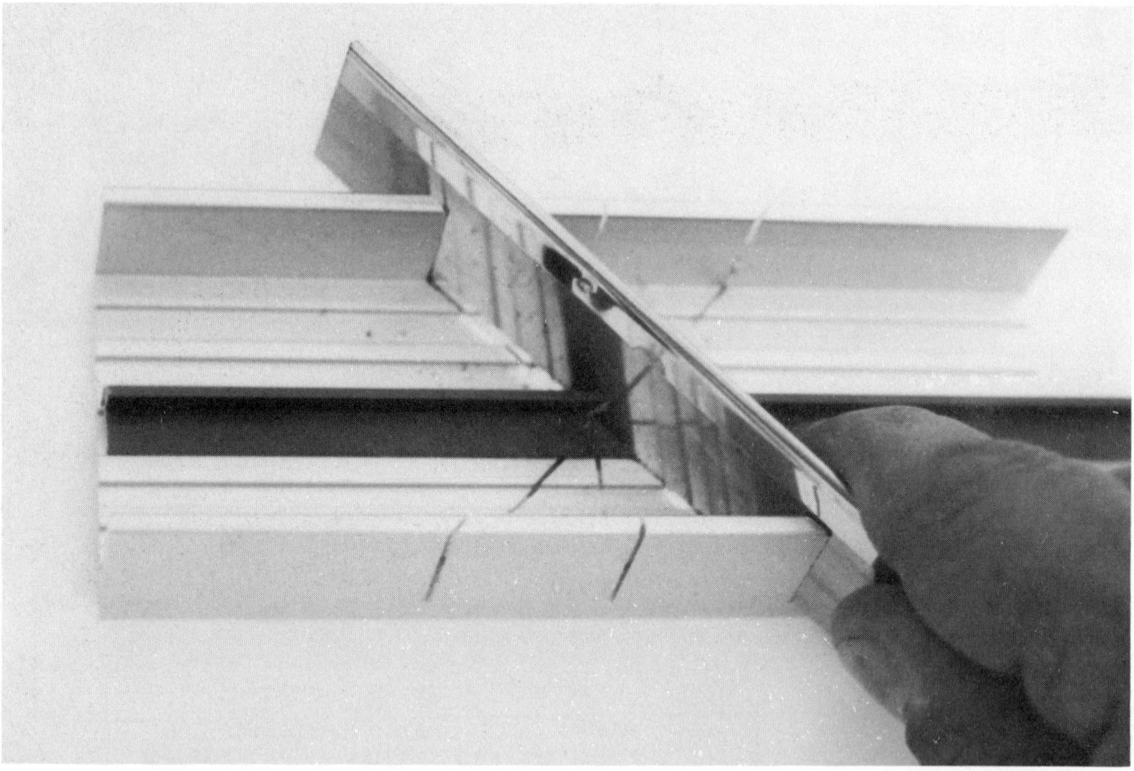

Fig. 6-14. For angle cutting, the X-acto miter box is a necessity.

Fig. 6-15. After cutting, pieces are aligned on schematic pinned in place and glued.

Fig. 6-16. Bottom girder must be notched to achieve proper girder fit.

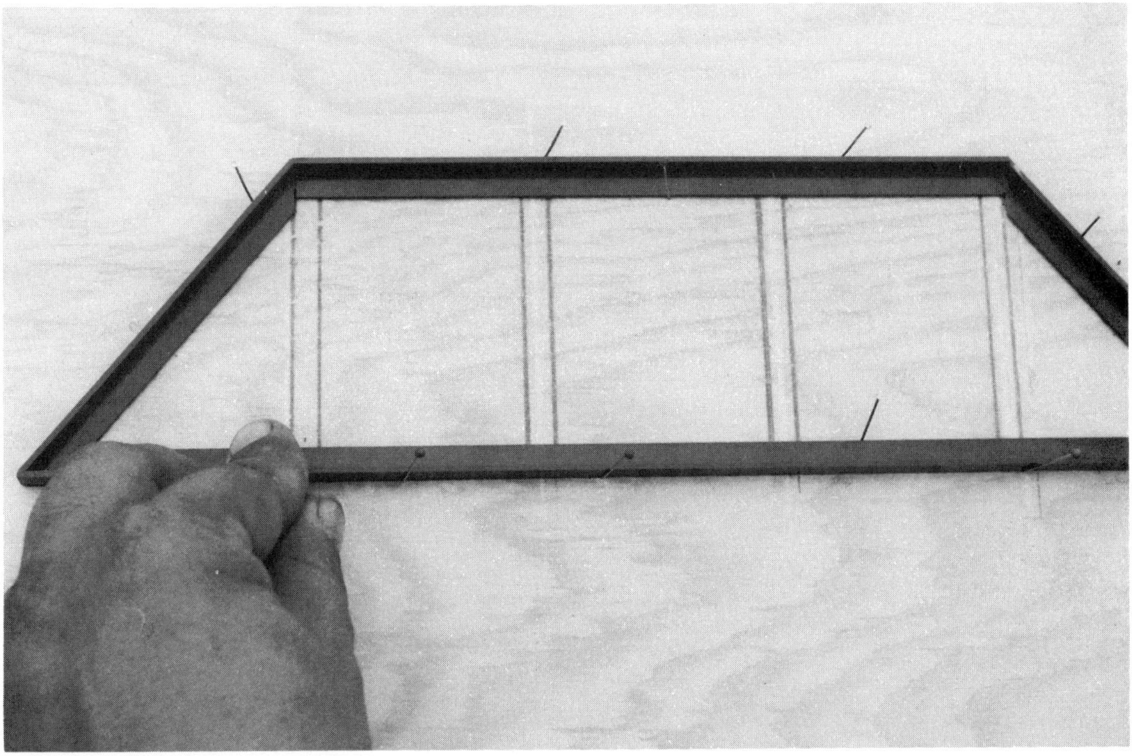

Fig. 6-17. Bottom girder is attached.

Fig. 6-18. Side girders are placed.

Fig. 6-19. Central "X" bracing and gussets are added, and one side is completed. Construct opposite side by repeating the entire procedure. Join the two sides with girder spans and the bridge is complete.

Chapter 7

Scenic Additives

(Courtesy Campbell Scale Models)

No matter how authentic, no matter how real-istically detailed, the model railroad pike is no more than an illusion. We try to introduce the essence of realism, but trick effects and imagination play an important part in the conception of the model pike. No matter how large a layout is, if it were to be scaled up to actual size in real life it would cover an area of a few miles. What the modeler wishes to create is the illusion that the modeled pike is more expansive and far reaching. With trick effects and backdrops we can expand on the illusion, making it indiscernible to the casual observer.

Painted backdrops containing mountains, cities, and scenery add depth and distance to the layout, and fortify our illusion. Uncluttered trackwork and large radius curves also give the feeling of more space. Mountains built up from the tabletop to emulate real mountains would have to reach ceiling height, a dimension that would throw the entire layout out of proportion unless it was built in the basement of an office building. Yet with a little bit of ingenuity we can allow the mountains or hills to appear larger and more expansive. If a mountain is toward the rear of the layout, we can use smaller trees on the mountainside. Instead of using an HO scale house or structure on the hillside, we can use an N scale component. It will be smaller, but we expect objects in the distance to appear smaller.

BACKDROPS

I can't stress enough the importance of scenic backdrops; they do much to subdue the limitations of confined space. Very few of us are good enough artists that we can create foolproof and exacting backdrops, but the problem has been solved for us. Walthers has made available a magnificent selection of integrated background scenes under the trade name "Instant Horizons" (Fig. 7-1). These "Instant Horizons" are visual masterpieces and highly recommended to all model railroad scenery buffs. Contained within these 24- × -36-inch murals that can be joined together, are cities, freight yards, prairies, and deserts so finely rendered that they add depth and infinity to the pike—a necessary prerequisite for true realism.

Through the courtesy of Walthers Inc., we have reproduced from their catalog in Figs. 7-2 through 7-7, helpful mounting instructions and suggestions as to the proper use and placement of their backdrops in conjunction with tabletop scenery.

YARDS AND STRUCTURES

Structures go hand in hand with terrain and scenic effects to heighten the lifelike illusion. The structural components may be static or they can be working—motivated by electrical, electronic, or manual means. The remainder of this chapter will be devoted to a number of operational and structural facilities indigenous to most actual railroading locales and situations.

TURNTABLES

Turntables probably hold the most fascination for railroad modelers. On pikes containing steam locomotives they are almost a must because they were used universally to turn locos around for practical point-to-point operation. Though they are obsolete today, they were a mainstay of railroad operations of the steam era.

In Figs. 7-8 through 7-13 we encounter a true prototype situation. This facility is typical of most eastern turntables, built in 1928 and still in existence today, through inoperative. These photographs were taken in White River Junction, Vermont where the turntable is situated on "Roundhouse Road." Most turntables of the steam era were built along these lines with major or minor deviations governed by locale or the size of the motive equipment they jockeyed around.

Model railroaders are most fortunate today because there are a number of turntable kits available, some utilizing simple manual operation, some using motorized and highly sophisticated electronic indexing systems. Bowser markets a motorized drive and automatic indexing unit to go with their turntables that can also be purchased separately. The turntables feature simulated metal bridges in three sizes: 14 inch, 16 inch, and 18 inch. The turntables are of 1/2-inch plywood with a brass pit wall with pit rail already laid in place. The turntable

Fig. 7-1. Walthers "Instant Horizons" provide todays layout modeler superb, second-to-none backdrops depicting varied scenic situations.

comes completely wired. Track and bridge details must be purchased separately.

By far the best turntable kits available are from Diamond Scale Construction. Virtually all types of turntables are offered, from old-time 51-foot timber deck types to modern steel plate 135-foot units. Aside from the ultimate realistic detailing included, the Diamond Scale models are extremely easy to put together because the instruction sheets are so explicit and easy to follow. The solid state indexing kits obtainable with the kits or separately are the best-conceived units available and easy to put together with the aid of a good pencil soldering iron. Figure 7-14 shows the prefinished turntable pit the motor and linkage assemblies. Figure 7-15 shows the indexing mechanism kit and the solid state electronic unit, which is the "brain" of the working turntable.

Though the circuitry of the indexing may be complex, the operational features are simple; all the complexities have been taken care of by Diamond Scale. After the control unit is assembled, all the components are wired together as delineated in the instruction manual.

In operation, a turntable feeder track is selected by means of a rotary selector switch on the control box. A starter button is pressed and the bridge commences to rotate in the desired direction. The sensory rotor under the turntable revolves until it contacts the track sensor of the feeder track selected. Brief electrical contact takes place between the rotor and the first track sensor, slowing the rotating bridge to about 1/4 RPM. The bridge now rotates until the track sensor makes contact with a second sensor on the rotor, causing the circuit board to cut off power to the motor. The bridge

Scenes can be mounted directly on a smooth, flat wall, or on panels of masonite, linoleum, or plywood, which are then mounted behind the layout.

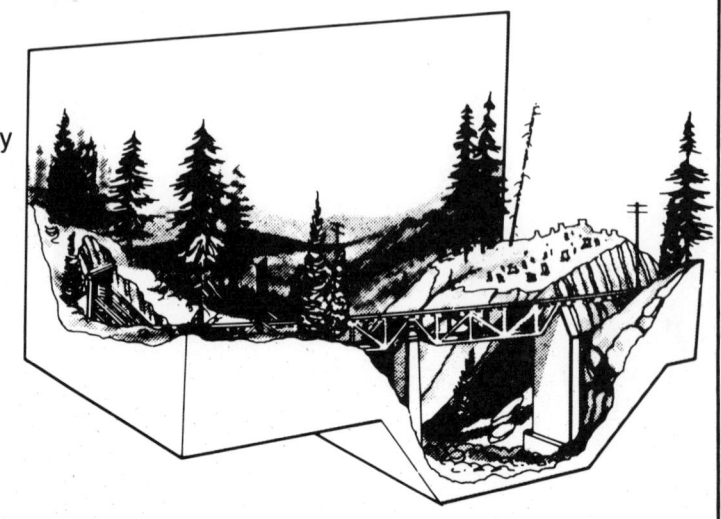

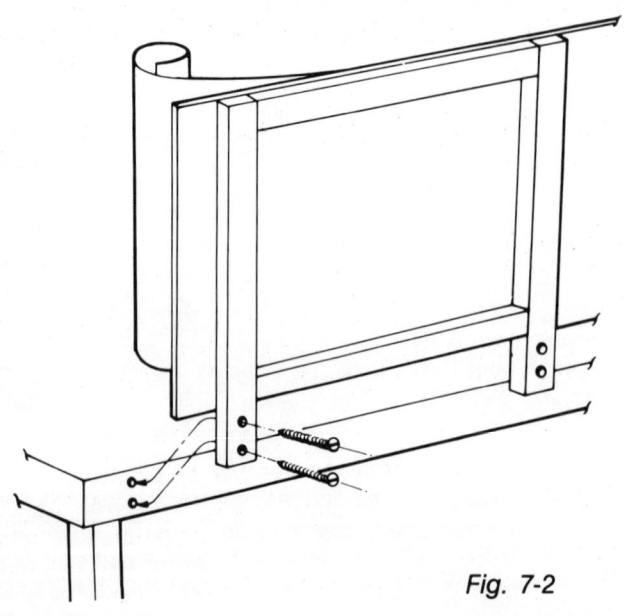

If mounted on panels, we recommend that these be seperate from the layout, as shown in the sketch. This makes it easier to remove the ''scenes-on-panels'' for work on the layout. A frame of 1″ × 2″ lumber can be used to provide stiffening, if needed.

Fig. 7-2

(Figures 7-2 through 7-7 Courtesy William K. Walters.)

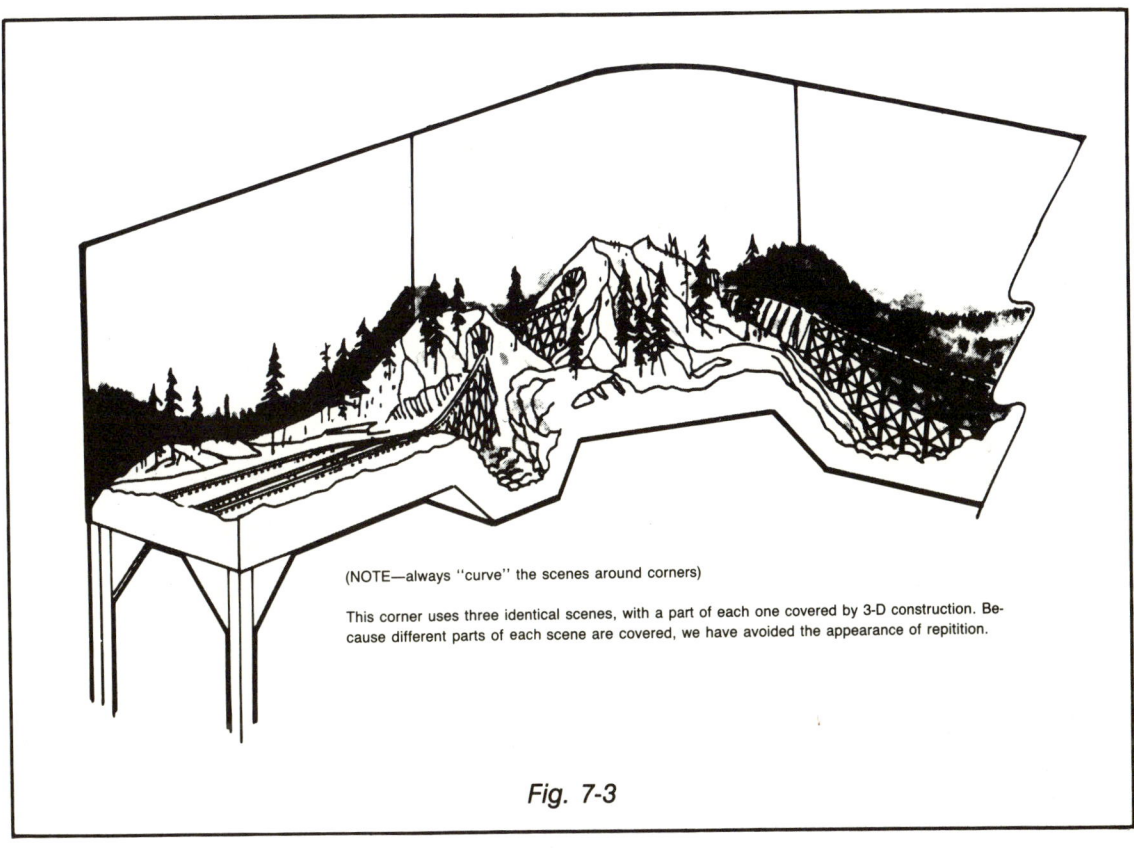

(NOTE—always "curve" the scenes around corners)

This corner uses three identical scenes, with a part of each one covered by 3-D construction. Because different parts of each scene are covered, we have avoided the appearance of repitition.

Fig. 7-3

drifts a fraction of an inch into positive alignment with the feeder track (or engine storage track). As the track sensor and rotor sensor maintain electrical contact, the control box indicator light turns on. This shows that the tracks are in exact alignment. No light means the tracks are not in alignment. Should this happen, the tracks can be aligned by jockeying the bridge back, using the jog button also found on the control box. Operation and assembly is so simple that one does not have to be at all electronically knowledgeable in order to put the turntable into perfect working order (Figs. 7-16, 7-17, 7-18).

Bridge and pit assembly is a snap, most of the parts are pre-fabbed and pre-cut, save for the bridge section in each turntable, which requires a minimal amount of construction expertise.

In most cases the addition of a turntable facility on the layout also justifies the inclusion of an enginehouse (straight stall or roundhouse). There are a number of these on the market—quite a few to be exact—both in plastic and in craftsman quality kits. A couple of the better ones are described in this chapter. One important factor must be considered when using a roundhouse or an engine housing facility with angled stalls. Make sure the angles of stalls in the structure chosen conform with the approach angles of the feeder or storage tracks around the turntable. It is far easier to place the tracks to conform to the engine house stall angles rather than vice versa. Sometimes situating the engine house closer or further from the turntable will also aid in achieving correct angles (Figs. 7-19 and 7-20).

YARD FACILITIES

Proper and adequate yard facilities are important and should augment the requirements of your motive power, environment, and locale modeled (Fig. 7-21).

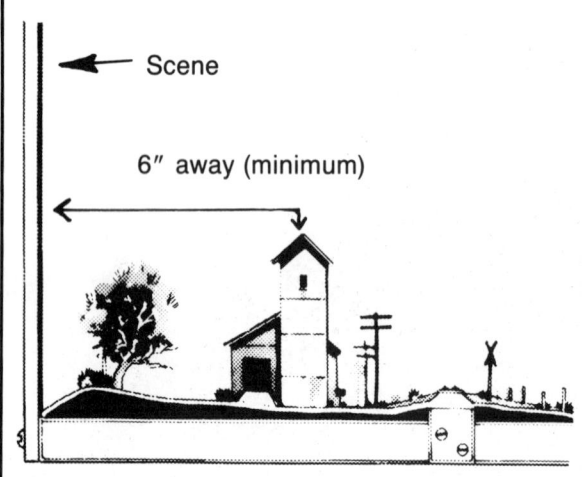

Scene

6″ away (minimum)

Large 3-D structures should not be any closer than about 6″. 12″ would be better and would heighten the illusion of depth and distance. (Keeping to this rule also helps eliminate unnatural shadows on the background scene.)

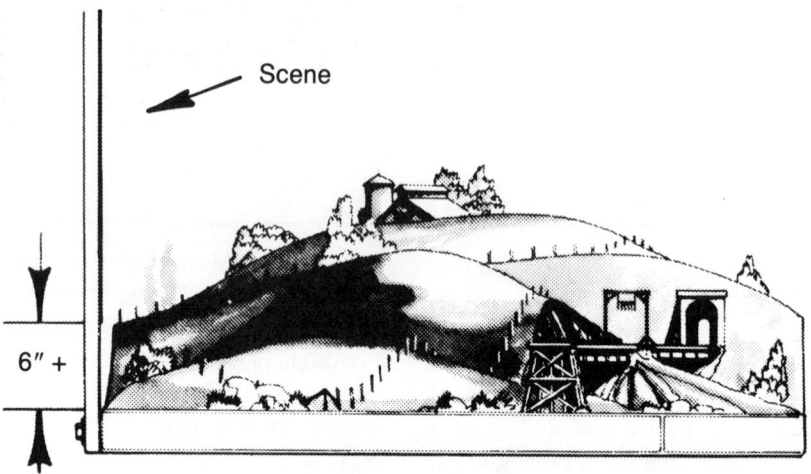

Scene

6″ +

These middleground hills represent typical rolling farmland. The background has been raised about 6 inches for added height and scenic effect. (The adjoining scenes must also be raised, or some alternate transition provided, of course.)

Fig. 7-4

In this sketch the 3-D mountain leads up to, actually touches, and blends into the background scene. The effect is most realistic when the colors from the 3-D scenery blend into the background scene coloring.

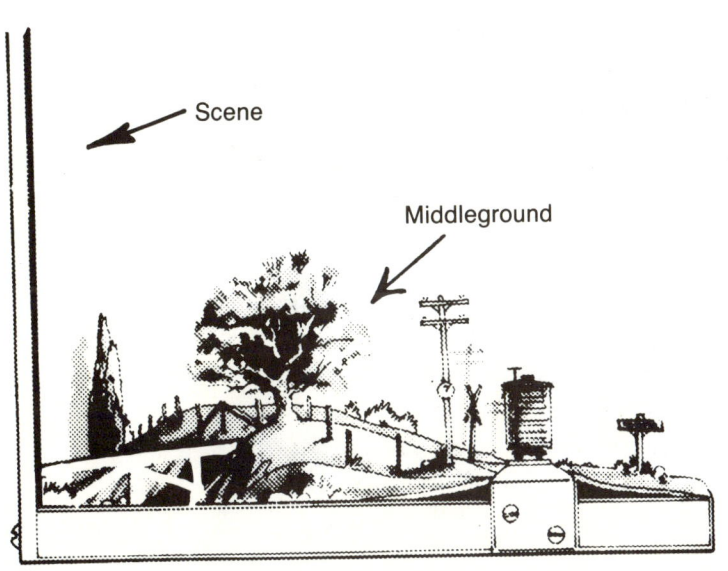

Fig. 7-5

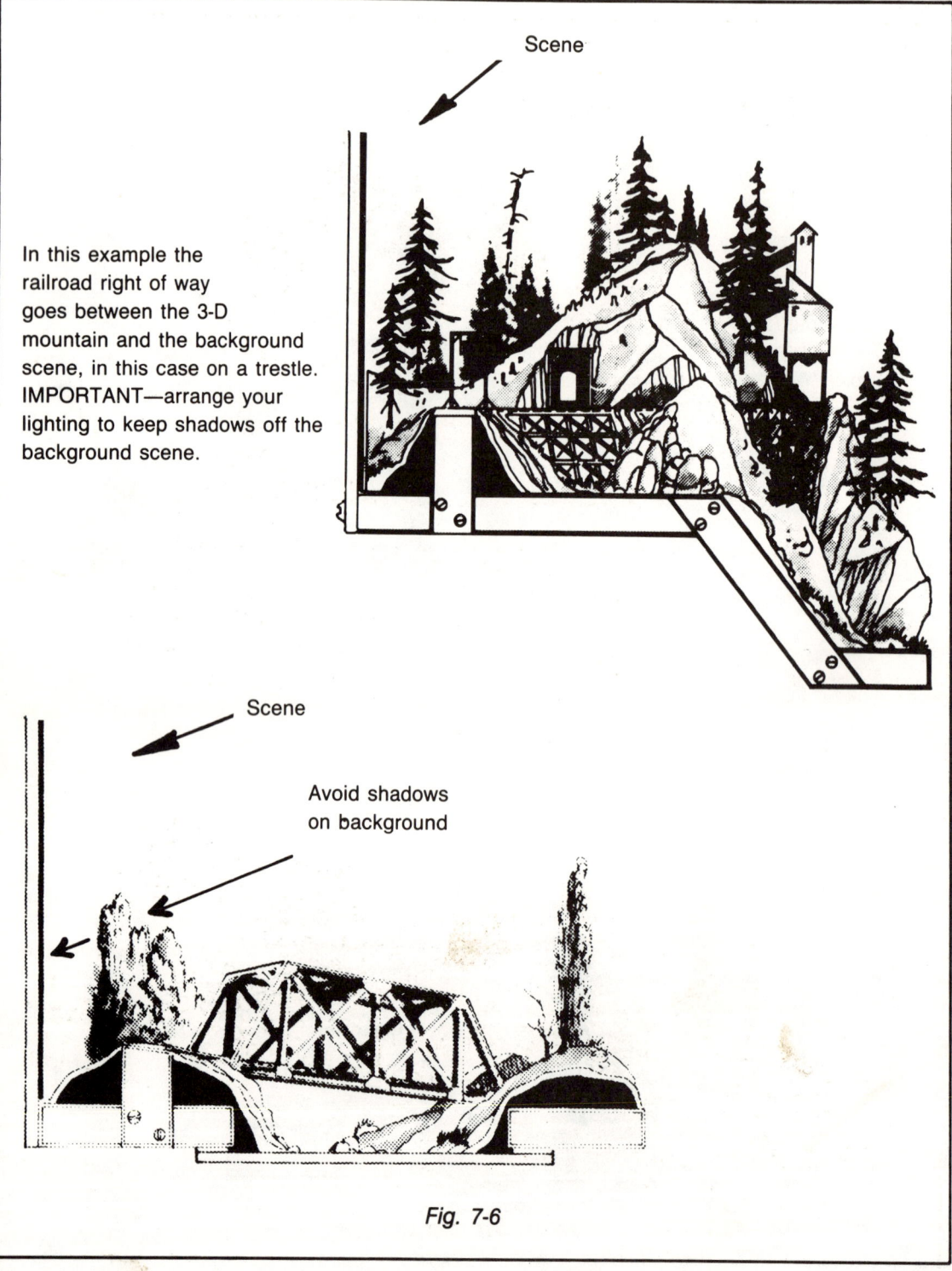

In this example the railroad right of way goes between the 3-D mountain and the background scene, in this case on a trestle. IMPORTANT—arrange your lighting to keep shadows off the background scene.

Scene

Scene

Avoid shadows on background

Fig. 7-6

Scene

Here the 3-D mountain is in front of (does not touch) the background scene. This maximizes the effect of perspective. the scene will actually look different when viewed from different parts of the layout. (Note that the 3-D mountain slopes DOWN into the background scene.)

Fig. 7-7

Fig. 7-8. An excellent example of a prototype turntable still in existence but not used. Locale: White River Junction, Vermont.

Fig. 7-9. Close-up of turntable bridge structure.

Fig. 7-10. Ring rail and pit wall.

Fig. 7-11. Bridge motivating mechanism.

Fig. 7-12. Roundhouse storage tracks. Foreground shows the end of bridge deck.

Fig. 7-13. Bridge alignment and locking device.

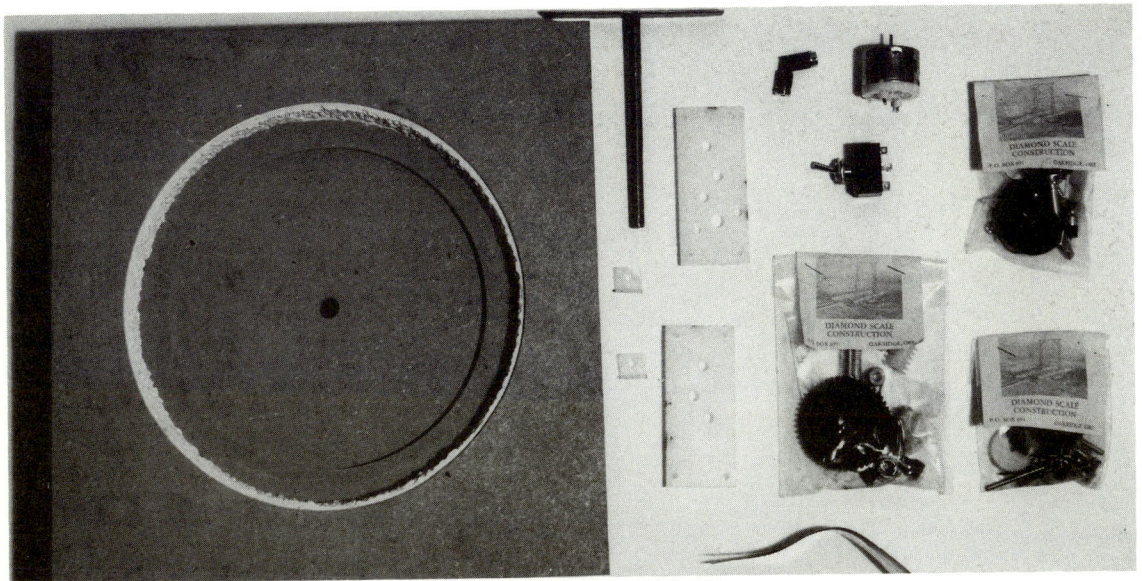

Fig. 7-14. The Diamond Scale old-time turntable and motor drive mechanisms.

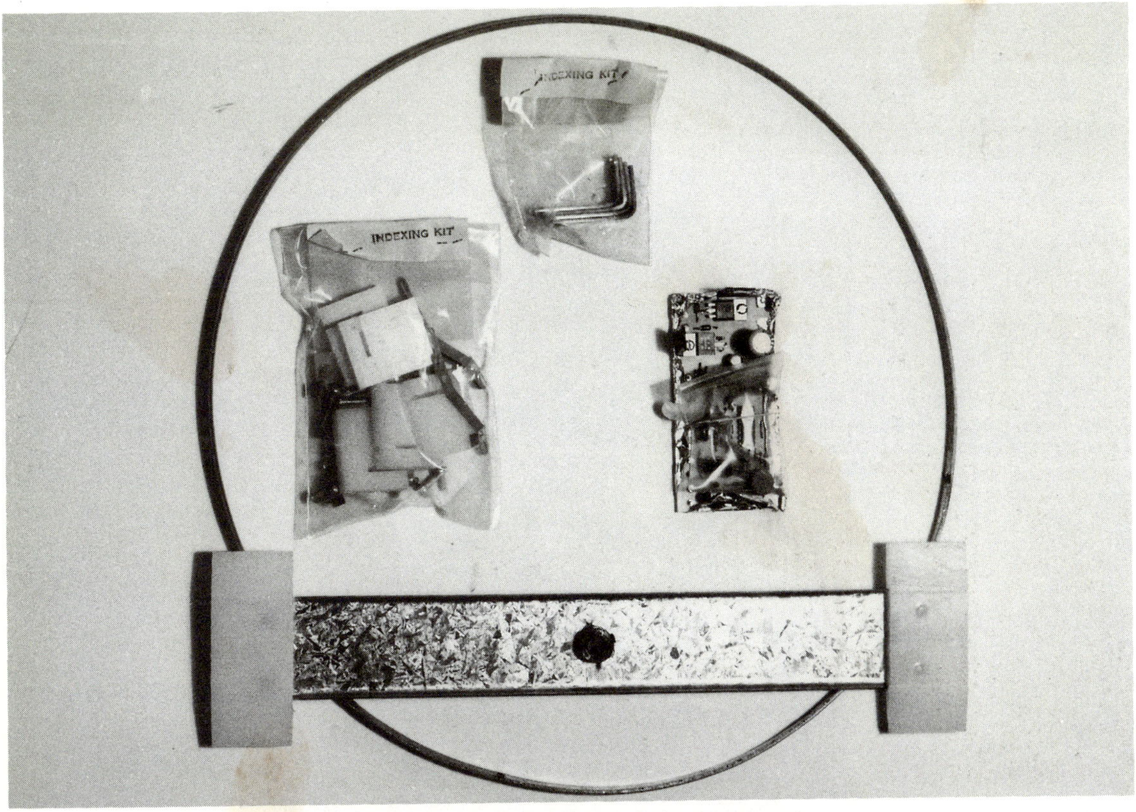

Fig. 7-15. Diamond Scale Sensory mechanisms and solid state indexing components.

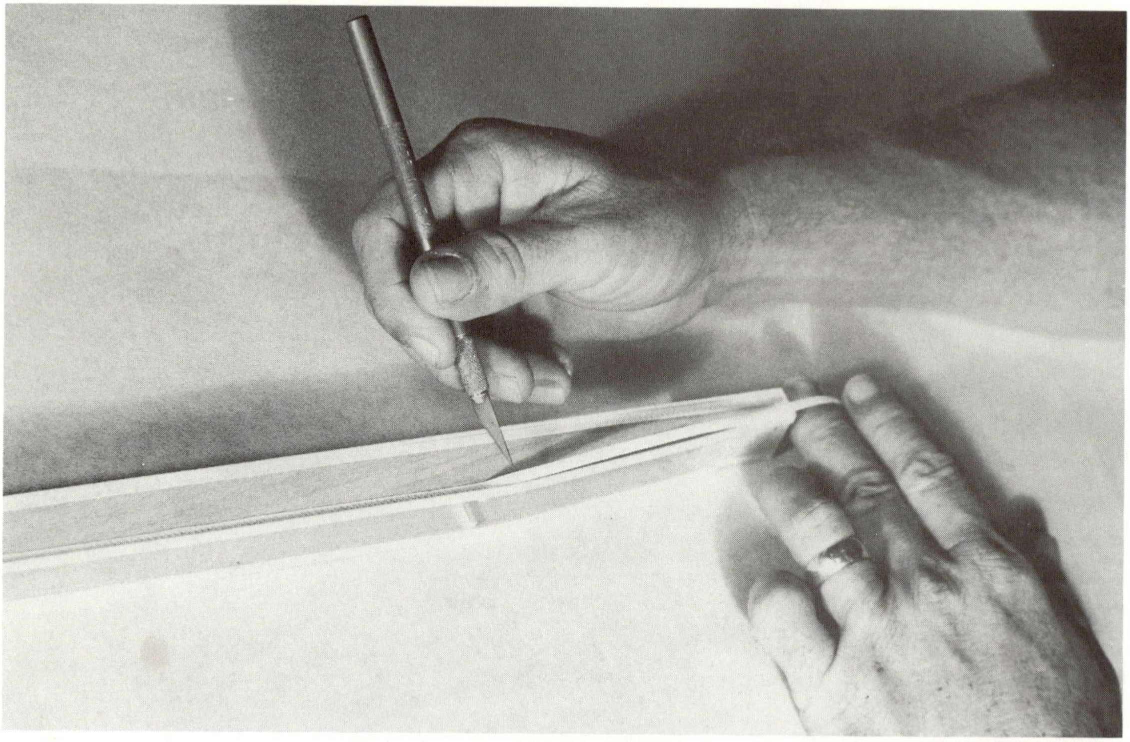

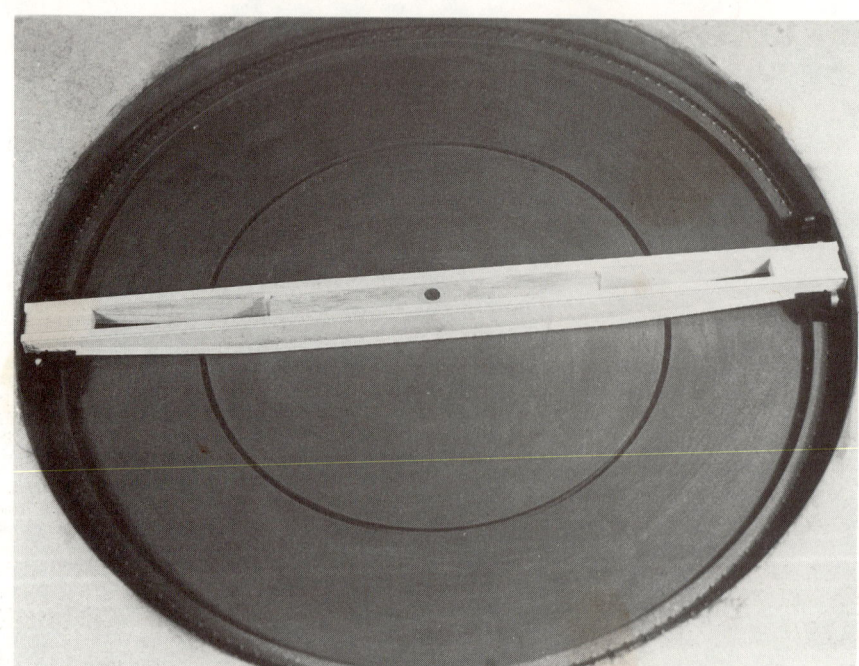

Fig. 7-16. The bridge on the Diamond Scale 135-foot turntable goes together easily with highly detailed components.

Fig. 7-17. The large Diamond Scale turntable with semi-finished bridge.

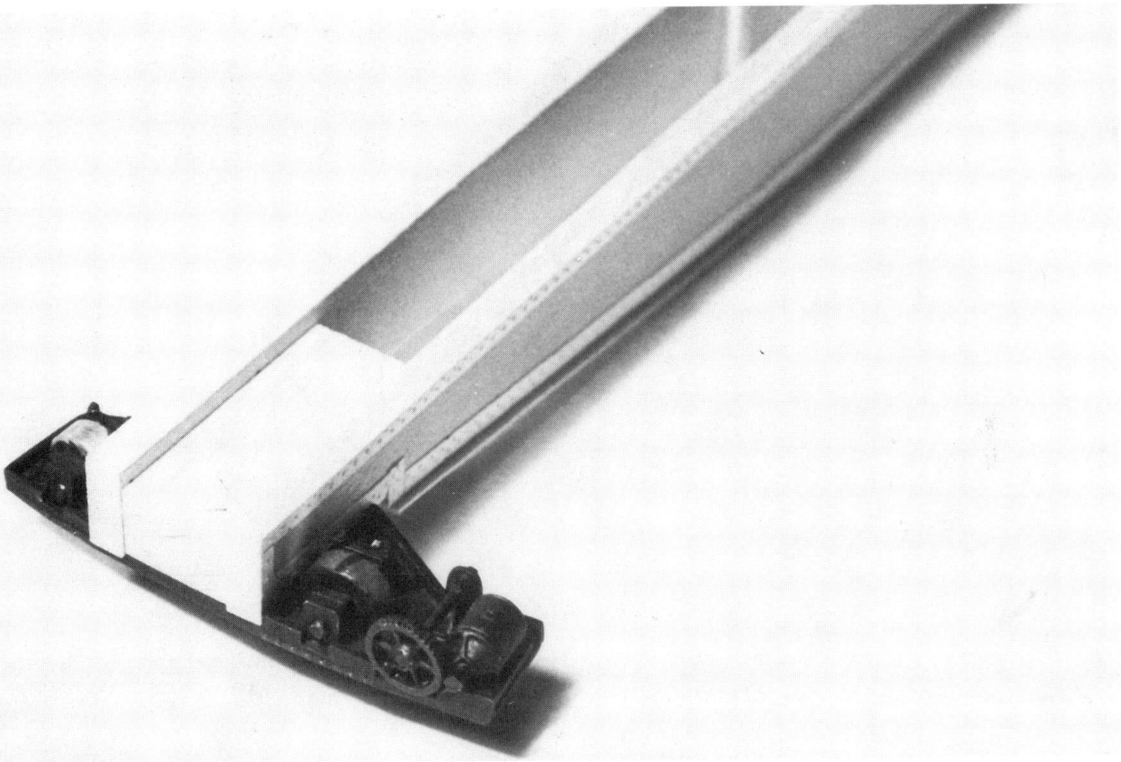

Fig. 7-18. Close-up view of driving motor casting exemplifies Diamond Scales attention to details.

Fig. 7-19. An excellent branchline engine house by Campbell. (Courtesy Campbell Scale Models)

Fig. 7-20. This unusual and distinctive three-stall engine house is offered by Detail Associates. (Courtesy Detail Associates)

Fig. 7-21. Good design sense and excellent modeling are the key in yard design planning. (Courtesy Lauderdale Shore Line Model R.R. Club)

Don't put a coaling tower on your layout if you are running woodburning or oil burning locomotives. If you are running primarily steam locomotives, make sure you include coal or oil towers, and watering and sanding facilities somewhere along the right of way or in the yards (Figs. 7-22, 7-23). Large yards will give you an excuse to model and place cinder drops, coaling facilities, water towers, and sand houses all in the same proximity—giving the yard a busy as well as a functional and balanced look.

Don't place open top water towers (even though they might be different and distinctive) in the middle of a desert where it never rains and the sun

Fig. 7-22. A totally different and distinctive water tower by Detail Associates. (Courtesy of Detail Associates)

Fig. 7-23. Northern locales featured enclosed water structures such as this Northerner by Campbell Scale Models. (Courtesy Campbell Scale Models)

evaporates water. Yard facilities should never exhibit a new look. They should show dirt, grime, and wear from constant usage (see Chapter 10: Painting and Weathering). To avoid a static look, include some working structures or models powered by small motors or electronic gimmickry in your yards (Fig. 7-24).

The key to realism is simulated authenticity. Though the model railroading illusion must work somewhat in conjunction with the imagination, model to the most infinite degree possible. The less you leave to the imagination, the closer you approach authenticity, and consequently, realism.

Fig. 7-24. The Campbell Quincy travelling crane adds activity to any yard situation. (Courtesy Campbell Scale Models)

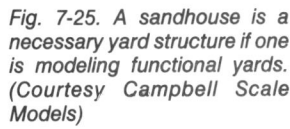

Fig. 7-25. A sandhouse is a necessary yard structure if one is modeling functional yards. (Courtesy Campbell Scale Models)

Fig. 7-26. Don't neglect people; they make situations more credible. This is a Weston engineer at home in both steam or diesel cabs.

Chapter 8

Individualization

The sophisticated terminology is individualization; pet railroad jargon labels it kitbashing. Either way it means major or minor structural or additive deviations to a stock or standard kit—be it a yard structure, house, building, or rolling stock. Of course the kitbashing must be done in good taste; you wouldn't put a wooden roof on a brick building or a wood framed porch on a stone house.

Kitbashing serves two major functions: to change the appearance so that the model differs from another out-of-the-box entity and to add details that are not included, which when added would improve and upgrade the overall look. Some people might want to take a vintage building for example, and modernize it in the same mode that actual buildings are refurbished. This can easily be done by putting on a modern roof, adding modern windows, stacks, ventilators, etc. One can utilize a multitude of available scale castings for modifications or fabricate parts or additives by hand. Check the additive and superdetailing parts section of the Walthers catalog. Here you will find offerings of all the major detailing parts manufacturers. Just about anything is available. Multitudes of doors, windows, people, tooling, furniture—you name it and it's there.

Detailing parts are usually cast in plastic, brass, or zamac. Plastic parts feature fine detailing and are easy to secure with styrene or Duco Cement. Brass (lost wax castings) parts are very detailed and may be affixed with epoxy (to any surface) or solder (to brass or metal). Zamac (zinc alloy) is rougher than brass or plastic and might have to be finished off a bit. Nevertheless, I have found some superbly detailed parts in zamac through the years, and they are sturdy and inexpensive to boot. Larger zamac parts might be heavy, but this is a negligible factor because we do not build railroad models from paper.

Kitbashing will allow you to model an existing kit to its infinite degree. I recall a situation in which I purchased what I considered to be the ultimate engine house. Going through the kit I found it to live up to every expectation. One thing bothered me, however. the walls were of vacuum-formed plastic to imitate stone, which were realistically ex-

cellent when painted. Somewhere along the line I had seen model stone wallwork that was superior. After a number of trips to some of the better hobby shops I frequent, I found just what I was looking for: a dynamite stone wall sheeting so detailed it gave the original kit offering secondary status. I substituted the improved styrene sheet version and was able to come up with a better-looking variation of an already magnificent structure. This is basically what individualization or kitbashing is all about.

A visual presentation will elaborate on this concept. The photo on page 101 shows a structure conceived and marketed by Durango Press and known as "Perkins Store." In the original plans, this structure is a multilevel building, allowing the modeler his own landscaping options. Here is how I kitbashed my model, which was built as a modular unit. (This is a good approach if one intends to dismantle or move the layout at a future date.)

Perkins Produce has the back wall and loading platform higher than the front, to allow the stone bottom unit of the structure to emanate from the ground at a lower level. In my version I built up a little hill around the left side of the structure (Fig. 8-1), going up to and serving as a base for the loading platform of the building. Plaster was used for all the groundwork. Simulated tire tracks were placed in the ground around the loading dock and cans and lumber fragments were scattered around. A pine tree was added to the left of the building and to liven up the diorama, as was a small cast plastic pond.

The building was weathered, as were the roof and windows—liberally sprayed (airbrushed) with Floquil Dust. Note in particular the billboard. In all the Perkins models I have seen (including the original plans) the billboard is perfect: clean, perfectly rectangular, straight. How often do we see billboards that are that perfect? Not often. After placing the decal, I soaked it with Solvaset to soften the decal film then manipulated the decal and edges until I obtained the degree of distortion you see in Fig. 8-1. The poster is also cocked a bit, torn in places, and dirt smudged. Roof shingles were weathered as described in Chapter 10 and stained

Fig. 8-1. Side one features lower level warehousing, massive tree, and backyard odds and ends.

as shown in the color section.

Figure 8-2 shows another facade of the building. The banks of the pond were built up to the staircase, which comes down to yet another level of ground. The stairway and crooked handrail were modeled to look rickety. A Woodland Scenics hardwood tree (right) was also added as a landscaping touch. The contrast between the full tree and the sparser, distinctively different pine tree also helps to balance the diorama. Figure 8-3 shows the remaining side of the structure. The platform sports irregularly placed boards, and the back window has been boarded up—different yet credible. The roof exhibits some torn and displaced shingling, which is very valid for shingled roofs.

Though this structure as it comes out of the box

is a superlative rendering of a general store, you can see at a glance what a little individualized detailing can do to enhance and improve a kit.

Rolling stock is also highly favored for kitbashing from mild to wild. In Fig. 8-4 we can study caboose configurations. The original kit was a Cliff Line Bobber as shown in the photo in the background. We removed and changed some windows, added a cast cupola and superdetailed the bobber until it evolved into the model shown at the right of the photo.

In Fig. 8-5 is another caboose rendering. Here modeler Doug Cline included a removable roof and upper compartment, plus inside wall details since the finished piece was to have a completely detailed interior. Doug's modeling expertise can also be

103

Fig. 8-2. Left side displays stairway pond and additive greenery.

studied in Fig. 8-6. Doug took two long tank car bodies, joined them together at the center to make one of the huge, extra-long, four-truck giant tankers prototypically produced but not available in kits. Projects like this separate the men from the boys. Unfortunately the model was incomplete at this writing, but you can study the basics and craft techniques involved.

If you will flip over to the color section of this book you will see a favorite rendering of mine, a wood-boom, steam-driven crane car—freelanced, but with some logic thrown in.

The foundation for the steam crane was an Ulrich Flat car of the older type to add the necessary character to the finished piece. The boom was scratchbuilt from basswood, brass shim stock (to

simulate metal platework), model ship single blocks, and carpet thread to serve as the cable. A vertical boiler and steam engine assembly were added behind the boom, and proper, detailed (brass wire) piping, valves, T's, and elbows were integrated according to typical steam engine and piping practices. The canopy is framed in wood, the roof is galvanized metal (scribed aluminum foil), the water tank is scratchbuilt tubing, the tank securing straps are shim stock detailed with Kemtron simulated scale nut and bolt ends.

Though the idea of the boom was lifted from an old *Carstens Rolling Stock Plan* book, the rest of the car was freelanced all the way. The model is over 20 years old, and the vertical boiler and steam engine kit is also dated—but if not available, a num-

Fig. 8-3. Back view: upper level detailing.

Fig. 8-4. Variation on a simple Bobber caboose.

Fig. 8-5. Model by Doug Cline features removable roof on cupola room.

Fig. 8-6. Ultra-long modern tank car by Doug Cline in its basic stage.

Fig. 8-7. Cal-Scale N scale trestle kitbashed up to an HO scale mini-trestle.

ber of similar offerings are presented in the Walthers catalog.

Study the overall and close-up photos of this semi-scratchbuilt car in the color section and you can see the possibilities and avenues open to the kitbasher of today who has a wealth of parts and options at his disposal.

Closing this chapter we can study a simple but effective kitbash. The original model is an exact-

ingly detailed small trestle kit by Cal-Scale. Unfortunately out of the box this trestle is only suitable for N scale or HO N 3 scale. The solution is simple, though double the cost. Two kits were bought and two trestle decks were mounted side by side on top of the pilings. Now we have (Fig. 8-7) a trestle capable of handling HO trackwork. It makes a handsome small trestle to dress up narrow waterways.

Fig. 8-8. Individually stained wood strips attached to a large cardboard tube and wrapped around brass wire from Detail Associates exhibit realism in this tank section of an incomplete water tower.

Fig. 8-9. Campbell shingle material, available in rolls, is a great additive detail medium.

Chapter 9

Superdetailing

In railroad modeling, superdetailing is considered the "art" of the craft. It is the addition of detailed additives and infinite embellishments (parts, castings, scratchbuilt components) that creates state-of-the-art reproduction.

The leaders in state-of-the-art modeling are the Japanese, closely followed by the Koreans. No one who has studied the quality brass offerings of the Far East can deny the infinite craftsmanship involved. Most of the reproductions presented display exacting hand construction and detailing, which is the reason why most Japanese and Korean brass is so expensive.

The average or cost-conscious enthusiast can achieve, if not as refined a rendition, at least an upgraded version of a standard budget-level offering with the addition of superdetailing parts—many of which are identical in quality to the fittings found on sophisticated brass equipment. Cal-Scale, one of the foremost producers of refined castings, offers a handsome assortment of superdetailing parts. These parts are much preferred for their excellent finish and extremely fine detail characteristics. Cal-Scale specializes in refined parts and fittings for steam locomotives and a host of other specialized projects.

Brass wiring and piping material can be obtained from Detail Associates, as can a wide array of fittings for diesel locomotives.

Parts for superdetailing may be commercially obtained or can be fabricated from scratch, using the brass or styrene stock pieces that are carried by most hobby shops. Though superdetailing in most instances requires precision workmanship, it can be tackled by the novice provided that he starts at the bottom and confines his initial endeavors to simplified modifications.

One can begin by adding marker lights to a caboose, for instance, or railings to the ends of passenger cars. Anyone with the aid of some glue or strong adhesive, can undertake these additions. If one is too timid to apply solder, many pieces or parts can be more than adequately affixed with the new two-part epoxies that offer a strong, permanent bond.

A great project for the beginning superdetailer is the addition of underbody (brake system) detailing. there are a host of underbody detailing parts available either separately or in packaged kit forms. Underbody detailing is easy to install and attractive when fully assembled, adding much detail and authenticity to rolling stock. The tooling necessary includes a needle-nose plier (for shaping and bending wire), a wire cutter, a pin vise, a good epoxy, and necessary brake system components. Cal-Scale makes a number of brake system kits, some of them offered in brass or plastic options. The brass kits are sturdier and less fragile. The beginner might want to tackle one of the plastic kits because they are easier to put together. They only require a simple styrene or plastic cement for total mounting and assembly.

Figure 9-1 shows the Cal-Scale AB Brake System in component kit form and fully assembled on a reefer underbody sill. The Cal-Scale kit is available in both plastic and brass; the brass cast version is illustrated here. All that must be added by the modeler is the wire piping and rod control connectors. Brass or metal wire will serve this purpose, obtainable at better hobby shops or through Detail Associates. Cal-Scale includes a detailed set of installation plans that are clear and easy to follow—making the job simple enough for even the novice to tackle.

Figure 9-2 shows yet another Cal-Scale brake system, one usually found on vintage and older rolling stock. This kit is the Westinghouse KC brake system and it is equally easy to install. In addition, Cal-Scale makes a Westinghouse "U" fittings set for standard era tenders, and a Westinghouse "PC" high-speed brake system for tenders or passenger cars.

Getting into locomotive detailing involves more care and patience; the more intricate work should be tackled after the modelmaker has attained some scratchbuilding expertise. Figure 9-3 shows some of the components available that can be used as additive or replacement parts on many of the simpler budget or domestic locomotives marketed today. In Figs. 9-4 and 9-5 we see a complete systems kit comprised of fittings that must be assembled as well as piped together, a more intricate approach that

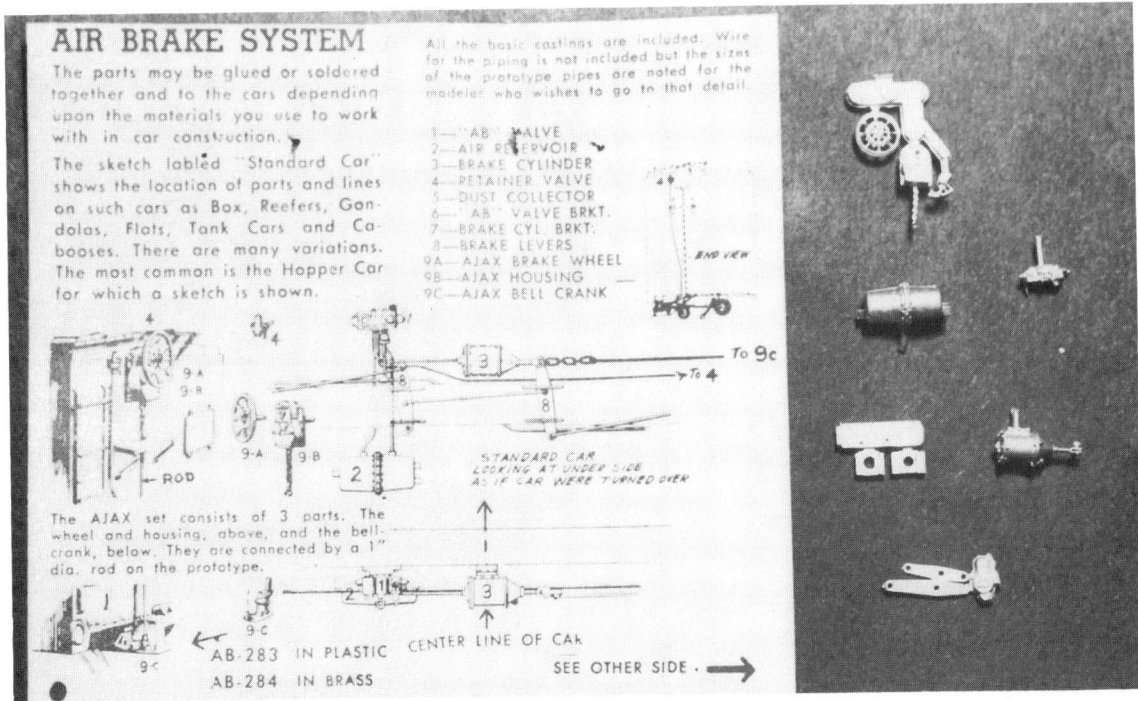

AIR BRAKE SYSTEM

The parts may be glued or soldered together and to the cars depending upon the materials you use to work with in car construction.

The sketch labled "Standard Car" shows the location of parts and lines on such cars as Box, Reefers, Gondolas, Flats, Tank Cars and Cabooses. There are many variations. The most common is the Hopper Car for which a sketch is shown.

All the basic castings are included. Wire for the piping is not included but the sizes of the prototype pipes are noted for the modeler who wishes to go to that detail.

1— "AB" VALVE
2— AIR RESERVOIR
3— BRAKE CYLINDER
4— RETAINER VALVE
5— DUST COLLECTOR
6— "AB" VALVE BRKT.
7— BRAKE CYL. BRKT.
8— BRAKE LEVERS
9A— AJAX BRAKE WHEEL
9B— AJAX HOUSING
9C— AJAX BELL CRANK

END VIEW

STANDARD CAR
LOOKING AT UNDER SIDE
AS IF CAR WERE TURNED OVER

The AJAX set consists of 3 parts. The wheel and housing, above, and the bellcrank, below. They are connected by a 1" dia. rod on the prototype.

CENTER LINE OF CAR

AB-283 IN PLASTIC
AB-284 IN BRASS

SEE OTHER SIDE ⟶

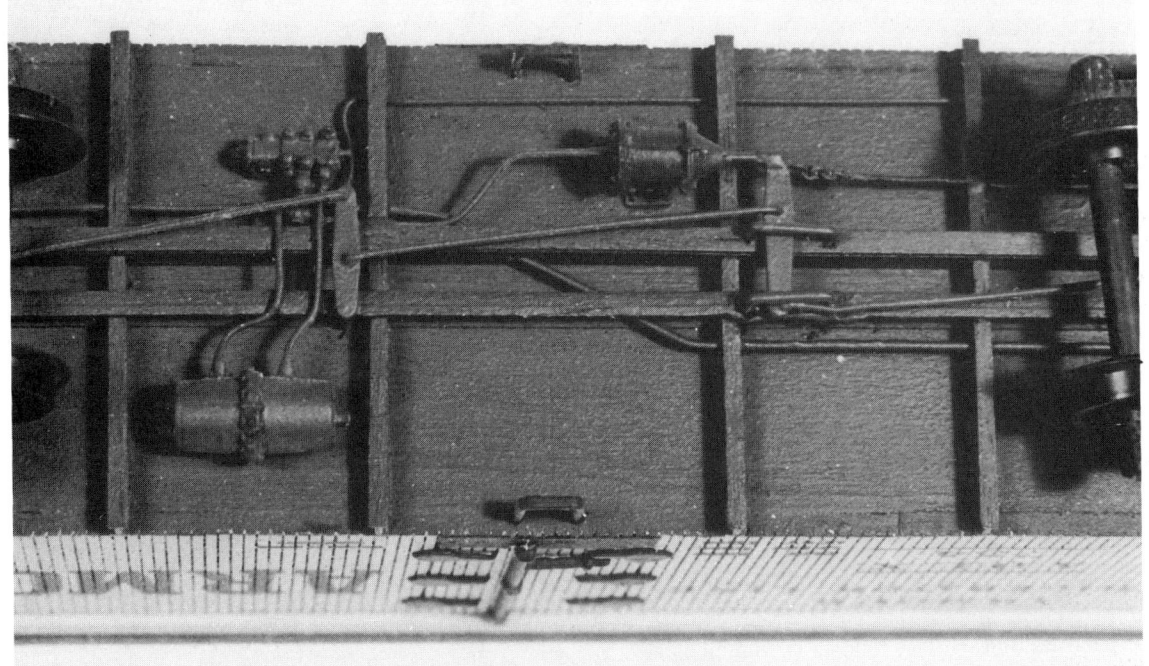

Fig. 9-1. Cal-Scale AB brake system (top) mounted on vintage reefer (bottom).

Fig. 9-2. Side view: Westinghouse KC system.

will be covered in a latter part of this chapter.

Not all locomotive additive detailing is complex. Some fittings can be attached with minimal skill. Some bells, for instance, can be mounted by just drilling a hole in the boiler and inserting the bell stem. Auxiliary domes and pop valves may be attached the same way. A simple glue-on (epoxy) additive is shown in Fig. 9-6. This is a detailed ashpan casting, the prototype of which was used on engines with small fire boxes up to the late 1930s. These ashpans are offered by Cal-Scale in pairs, one for each side of the fire box. If necessary, they may be cut down. Figure 9-7 shows the ashpan epoxied into place on a firebox. Note how detailing and dimension is added.

Headlights are easy to install and in most cases the superdetailed offerings available put the original cast-in appendages to shame. Washout plugs, though small, are easy to install, very detailed, and good looking when scattered around a loco boiler in their appropriate places. They are used on virtually all locos and can be mounted by drilling and epoxying. Check through the Cal-Scale and Kemtron catalog pages and you will find a wealth of glorifying additives. Once you have mastered placing and mounting simple fittings, you can move up to the more complex installations—such as the Elesco heater covered later.

DETAILING CONCEPTS

There are two valid approaches to locomotive detailing. The first follows prototype designation and specifications. This is the purists approach in which the modeler reproduces each and every detail. The second approach relies on the modeler's imagination and is referred to as the freelance

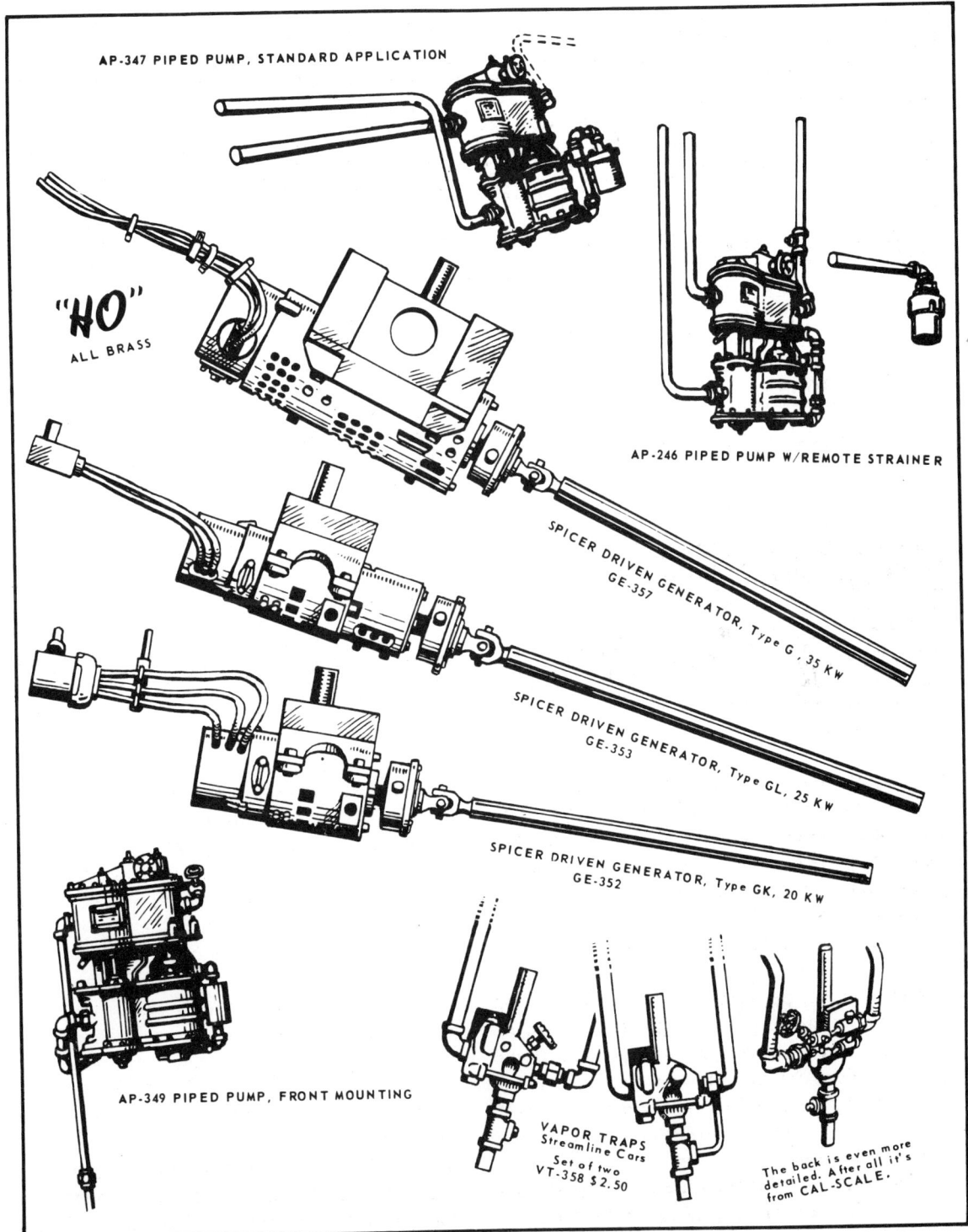

AP-347 PIPED PUMP, STANDARD APPLICATION

"HO"
ALL BRASS

AP-246 PIPED PUMP W/REMOTE STRAINER

SPICER DRIVEN GENERATOR, Type G, 35 KW
GE-357

SPICER DRIVEN GENERATOR, Type GL, 25 KW
GE-353

SPICER DRIVEN GENERATOR, Type GK, 20 KW
GE-352

AP-349 PIPED PUMP, FRONT MOUNTING

VAPOR TRAPS
Streamline Cars
Set of two
VT-358 $2.50

The back is even more
detailed. After all it's
from CAL-SCALE.

Fig. 9-3. Cal-Scale replacement parts. (Courtesy Cal-Scale)

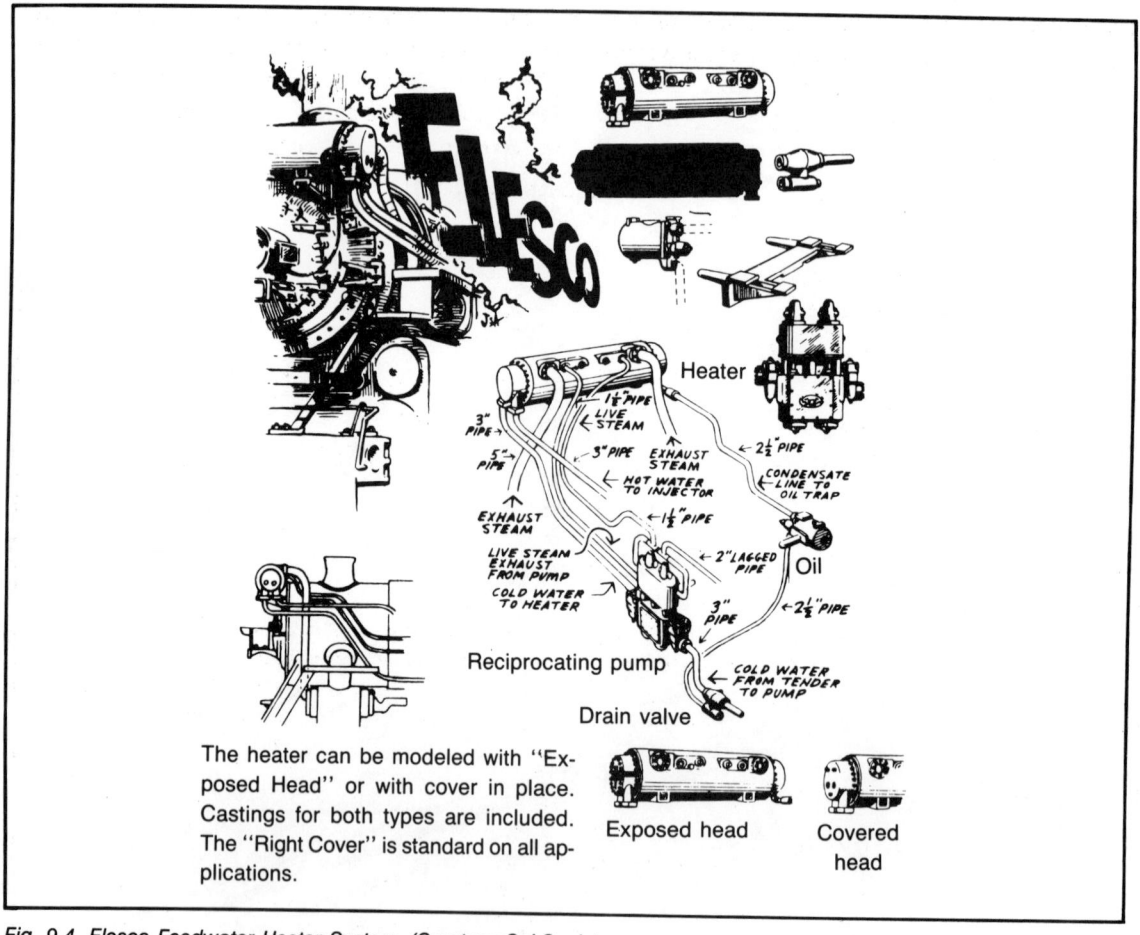

The heater can be modeled with "Exposed Head" or with cover in place. Castings for both types are included. The "Right Cover" is standard on all applications.

Fig. 9-4. Elesco Feedwater Heater System. (Courtesy Cal-Scale)

method. Some freelancers will design the entire locomotive from scratch, from the wheels and frame up. Others will take standard, obtainable locomotives and add or delete parts, or change and modify the detailing.

Purists and prototype duplicators frown upon the freelance approach. I feel it is as effective as following prototype practice, particularly if it is done with taste and good modeling sense. In many instances freelancing requires more knowledge and skill than necessary for prototype emulation. In order for a freelanced model to appear valid, the builder must know a great deal about accepted practices involving piping, generators, injectors, pumps, etc.—how the parts interrelate and their proper placement and order.

The best book available, and the bible of the locomotive craftsman is the *Model Railroader Cyclopedia, Vol. I: Steam Locomotives*, published by Kalmbach. No serious modeler should be without this magnificent volume, illustrating prototype practices and procedures as well as presenting scale plans of virtually every locomotive type from wood-burners to articulateds. A complete section of this volume is devoted to the parts of a steam locomotive and how they work, a valuable asset to the railroad modeler and enthusiast.

Once the modeler has gotten some basic super-detailing under his belt—such as the mounting of the simpler components as described in this chapter—he can delve into more intricate or more sophisticated additive approaches like piping, the

114

interrelated connections between many of the locomotive's working, and detailed structural components. To simulate piping, brass wire is most commonly used, but copper may also be utilized. The latter, however, is not as desirable or resilient.

Table 9-1 shows standard size piping (prototype) and the scaled-down wire equivalents. For larger pipe sizes it is best to utilize brass or copper tubing. In these cases copper will be easy to bend and conform to necessary shapes and angles.

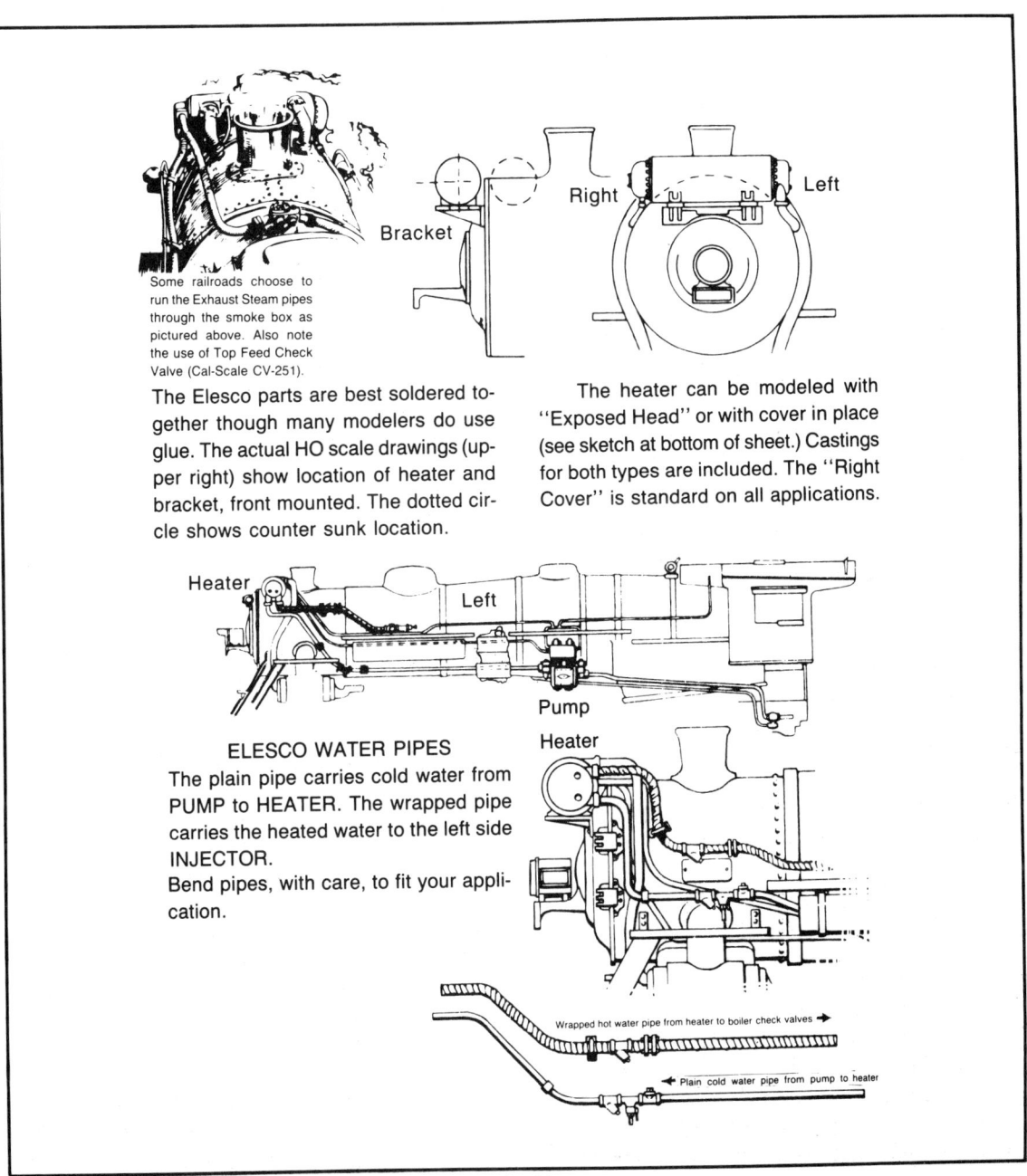

Some railroads choose to run the Exhaust Steam pipes through the smoke box as pictured above. Also note the use of Top Feed Check Valve (Cal-Scale CV-251).

The Elesco parts are best soldered together though many modelers do use glue. The actual HO scale drawings (upper right) show location of heater and bracket, front mounted. The dotted circle shows counter sunk location.

The heater can be modeled with "Exposed Head" or with cover in place (see sketch at bottom of sheet.) Castings for both types are included. The "Right Cover" is standard on all applications.

ELESCO WATER PIPES
The plain pipe carries cold water from PUMP to HEATER. The wrapped pipe carries the heated water to the left side INJECTOR.
Bend pipes, with care, to fit your application.

Wrapped hot water pipe from heater to boiler check valves ➤

◄ Plain cold water pipe from pump to heater

Fig. 9-5. Elesco Feedwater Heater System. (Courtesy Cal-Scale)

Fig. 9-6. Cal-Scale ashpan details.

Fig. 9-7. Ashpan details mounted in place on loco firebox.

There are standard piping procedures practiced in prototype situations and they should be followed closely in scale duplication:

- Horizontal piping is, in most cases, fastened closely against the sides of the locomotive. A great amount of piping is fastened below the running boards; above the running boards it should run close against the boiler.
- Model piping is secured with simulated clamps or brackets, fittings that are readily available from Cal-Scale or other fitting manufacturers.
- Vertical piping is installed first, then horizontal is installed over the vertical. Following this practice also when modeling will assist in simplifying piping assembly.

- Avoid severe right angle bends; wide radius bends are more preferable and prototypical. A standard practice is to keep the radius of the bend three times the width of the pipe (or wire).

Table 9-1. Piping Sizes For Prototypes And Scaled-Down Equivalents.

Prototype Width	HO Brass Equivalent
1/2″	No. 35
1″	No. 29
1 1/2″	No. 25
2″	No. 23
2 1/2″	No. 21
3″	No. 19
4″	No. 17

116

- Keep horizontal piping as straight and as parallel as possible. If the opposing ends of horizontal piping are to be at differing levels, the increase in rise should be instituted somewhere along the horizontal, utilizing 45-degree (or better) bends as frequently as required in order to accomplish the complete level change.

For the neophyte superdetailer embarking on his first piping and component installation, I would recommend adding an Elesco feedwater heater system which was universally used on many Mikados, Pacifics, T & P 2-10-4's, USRA Mountains, and N.Y.C. Lima L3b's.

Featured in this chapter is the Cal-Scale Elesco feedwater system with installation diagrams courtesy of Cal-Scale. Mounting and assembling this system is relatively simple.

The Elesco systems were mounted on locomotives, usually ahead of the smokestack, recessed into the boiler or on the uppermost part of the smokebox (front of boiler). The latter is the simpler of the two installations, and Cal-Scale provides special brackets that can be mounted on the smokebox.

In prototype situations, the tank houses a number of tubes for containing traversing water. Exhaust steam originating from the main cylinders and a special pump is piped in around these tubes. Sometimes there will be a special connection involved so that live steam can be routed to the heater when there is insufficient exhaust for proper heating (like when the locomotive is immobile) or freezing climatic conditions prevail. In the tank, the pumped steam or exhaust heats the boiler water, but does not mingle with it because the water is isolated by the tank piping. Condensed steam then drains (through piping, along the right side of the loco, crossing over under the boiler) into a water pipe at the rear (left side) of the engine. Before crossing over the engine under the boiler, the pipe feeds into an oil separator which keeps oil from infiltrating into the water supply and prevents steam formation in the boiler.

There are a number of variations of boiler-water connections to the heater that can be modeled. Cal-Scale presents and illustrates these variances with optional fittings for varied mounting procedures.

Prior to mounting and piping the Elesco system, the tank must be assembled, which can be a tricky "new" project for the fainthearted. Because this is the most complex aspect of the Elesco system construction, I will show step by step how the tank is assembled. First, the chosen end covers are snipped from the casting cluster. Two left side covers are offered, giving the detailer the option of modeling the exposed or covered head tank—both types were used commonly (refer to Fig. 9-4).

In Fig. 9-8 the Elesco tank body is mounted in an instrument vise to secure it as shown. The right side cover is put into place and pressure from the soldering iron tip is used to keep the cover in place. Wire solder is inserted into the tank from the opposite end, and the heat button on the gun is pressed, heating the gun tip. Make sure the tip of the iron or gun is free of any solder or it will transfer to the cover and mar the surface, obscuring the cast-in detailing. When the right temperature is reached, the solder will flow *inside* the tank and secure the side cover from the inside. It is important that an excessive amount of solder does not flow, because it will run out the opposite end or through the side cover seam.

The opposite cover is mounted. Again, the same procedure is followed: the tip is held against the cover and some of the solder inside the tank will flow back toward the second cover and secure it (Fig. 9-9).

The mounting bracket must then be attached. The bracket ends should be tinned, and the bracket is placed on the two tank blocks that mount to the bracket. Heat is applied until the solder melts and the bracket is allowed to cool while held in place (Fig. 9-10). Excess solder can be trimmed or scraped away if necessary (Fig. 9-11). Figure 9-12 shows the assembled tank unit.

Next, two holes must be drilled into the smokebox cover with a 1/32-inch drill bit (Fig. 9-13). The tank bracket tabs are inserted into the holes drilled into the cover and solder-secured from the rear of

Fig. 9-8. Securing right side cover: Elesco tank.

Fig. 9-9. Securing left cover.

Fig. 9-10. Soldering bracket onto tank.

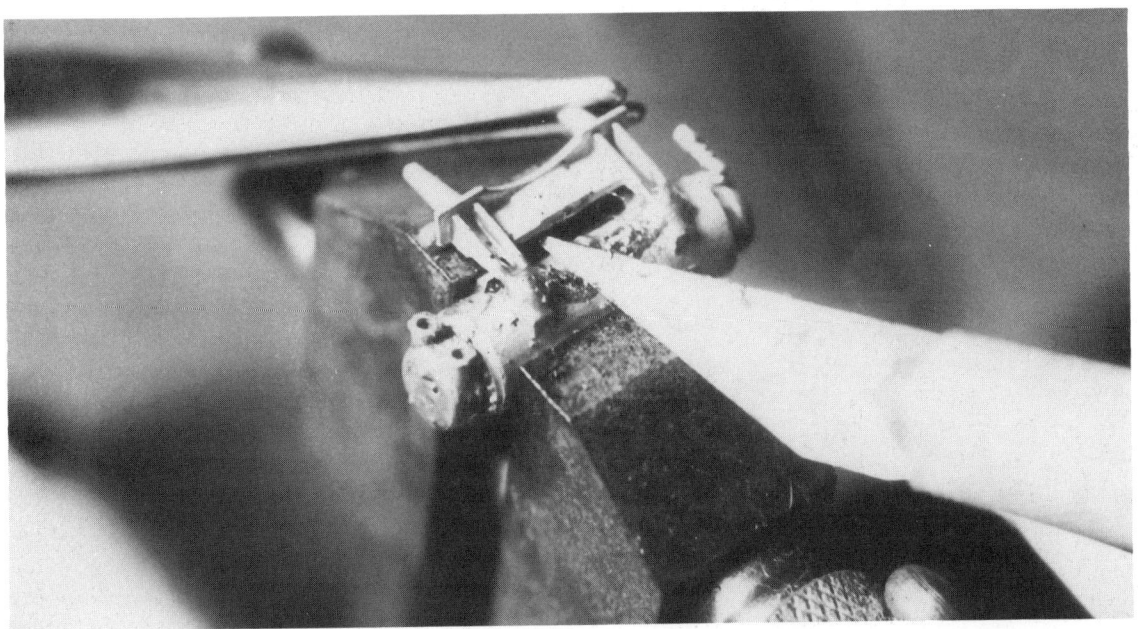

Fig. 9-11. Cleaning off excess solder.

Fig. 9-12. The assembled tank.

the cover (Fig. 9-14). Figure 9-15 shows the tank mounted in place. Mounting and assembling the tank is the most tedious part of the Elesco feedwater installation, but need not be an arduous task if care and patience are exercised.

Other small construction tasks similar to the Elesco installation will be within the modeler's grasp once he has gained some proficiency and skill with the simple tools and the soldering iron. Figure 9-16 shows an injector installation on an 0-6-0 switcher. Note also the washout plugs we spoke of before (circular recessed plates on top of injector).

Figure 9-17 shows a scratchbuilt superdetailed wooden gondola. Brake, wheel, ladders, and grab irons are all commercial castings. The stake pockets are pre-formed punched brass parts and are available from Kemtron. The interior of the gondola was also detailed using scribed Northeastern basswood (Fig. 9-18). Figure 9-19 shows a typical poultry car. Screening for the wire screen sides was simulated with kitchen curtain cloth; horizontal bars with heavy carpet thread.

There are a wealth of components and parts marketed for scratchbuilding and superdetailing today; how they are applied and implemented depends on the ingenuity and expertise of the modeler. Following are some examples of some refined superdetail work, both scratch and additive.

Fig. 9-13. Drilling holes for tank bracket mounting.

Fig. 9-14. Soldering bracket to smokebox cover.

One of the engines with traditional lasting charisma is the B & O Dockside. A small 0-2-0 switcher, the Dockside was adopted for barge loading and shunting activities on the docks serviced by the Baltimore & Ohio R. R. in the early and mid 1900s. HO model railroaders have enjoyed many scale offerings of this cute and popular mini steam locomotive. Varney manufactured the first offerings and was followed in the 1950s by Rivarossi. On the heels of the Rivarossi version came the ultra-superdetailed Sakura model in brass from Japan, the finest rendition ever offered, and hard to find today. Lou Kozla, an avid model railroader in south Florida, obtained one of these models and in Fig. 9-20 we see one individually stylized and detailed by Lou.

Even today, Kemtron, a leading producer of brass castings, markets a cab forward casting for

Fig. 9-15. Elesco tank affixed to smokebox cover

Fig. 9-16. Superdetailed roundhouse 0-6-0 switcher.

adapting the Dockside to a cab forward loco. To do this, Kozla cut off the rear facing of the Dockside cab and soldered on the Kemtron casting, adding on a reservoir tank, a bell, and an operative Kadee coupler. The seams were filled in and finished off to make a professional-looking modification in keeping with the exacting detailing of the

Sakura engine. To turn the short operational run Dockside into a long run loco, Kozla added a shorty Vanderbuilt tender. The tender was constructed from an old Kemtron tender kit no longer in production.

Those interested in emulating this model may still obtain the cab forward casting from Kemtron,

Fig. 9-17. Scratchbuilt, detailed wooden old-time Gondola.

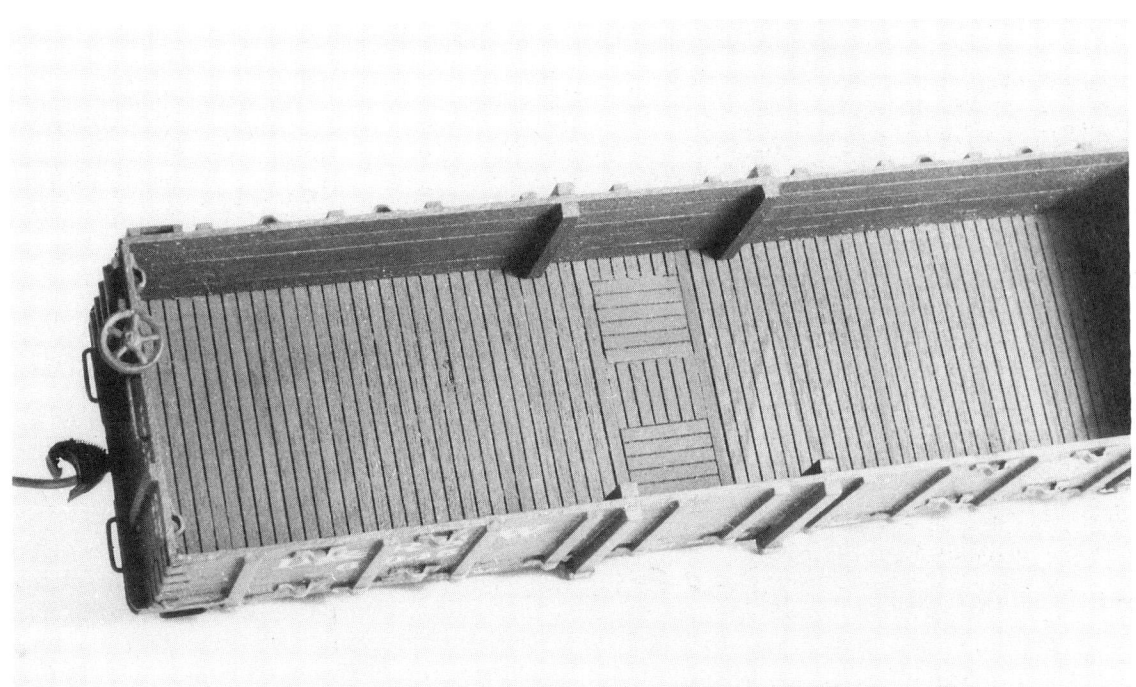

Fig. 9-18. Interior details: wood gondola.

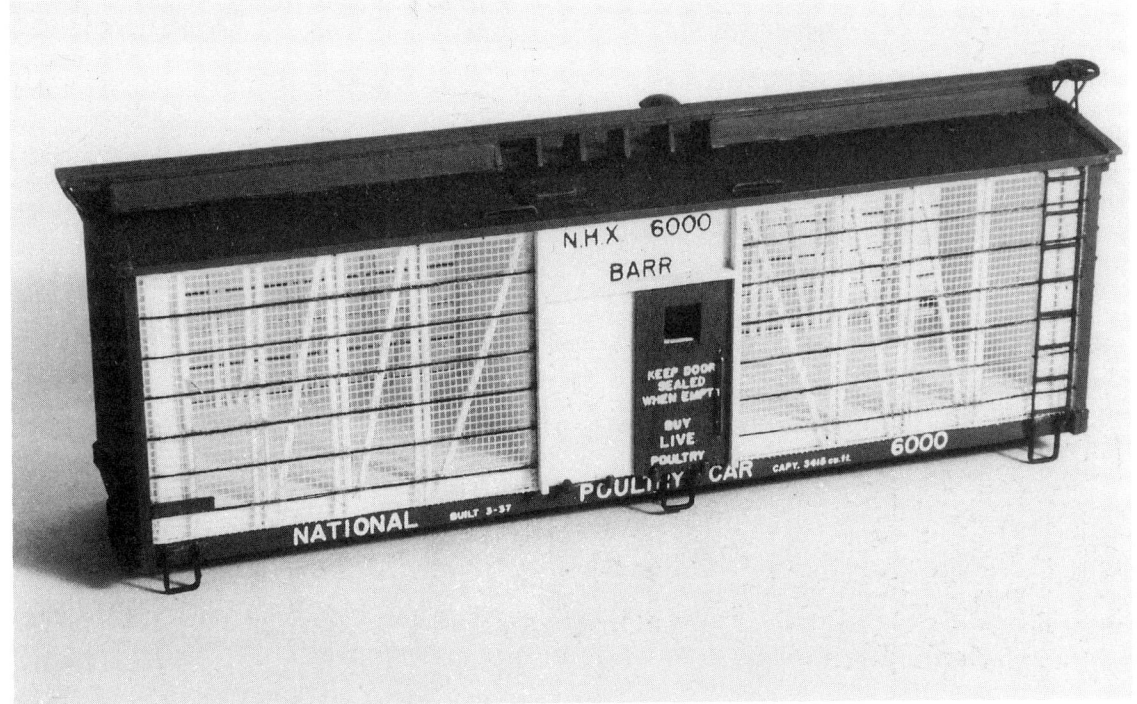

Fig. 9-19. Poultry car detailed as described in text.

and with a little cutting and shaping can realize a similar rendering. Walthers markets a few shorty Vanderbuilt tenders, which can be found in their catalog. The last manufacturer of the Dockside was Pemco, who are out of business. Some Pemco Docksides may still be obtained by modelers willing to check the better, well-supplied hobby shops. The Pemco versions are plastic and the brass Kemtron casting may be affixed using good grade, medium-drying epoxy cement. Kozla's model shown in the photo was finish painted in Floquil engine black, applied with an airbrush.

Modern motive power buffs can eyeball Hal Jerns upgraded GP50, fully glamorized with a host of superdetailing parts (Fig. 9-21). Jerns model was painted and decorated in Burlington Northern decor using Poly S colors (airbrushed) and Walthers decals (Fig. 9-22). Of particular detailing interest is the nose section of the diesel. The original pilot was deleted in favor of a snow plow type pilot available from Details West (or Walthers, which stocks Details West parts). Figure 9-23 shows the detailed pilot up close. A Kadee coupler was added as well as brass cast airlines. Air and brake line castings are marketed by Cal-Scale, Detail Associates, and

Fig. 9-20. Dockside cab forward: Sakura model, super-detailed and converted by Lou Kozla.

Fig. 9-21. Hal Jerns GP50.

124

Fig. 9-22. Hal Jerns GP50: decor and decals.

Kemtron—to name a few. All may be obtained from hobby shops dealing with Walthers Inc.

Figure 9-24 shows a scratchbuilt vinegar tank car that I built. Original plans are from an old, old *Model Railroader* magazine. It's amazing what can evolve from simple scratchbuilders parts.

Though the use of materials can be optional, the car shown here was built completely of wood,

brass wire stock, and brass shim stock. Everything was glued together except for some soldering on the wire straps and hand rail, mainly for joining the hoops and rails. The ladder is from brass ladder stock; grabirons and steps were hand bent and cut from brass wire. Turnbuckles are pre-formed parts (Kemtron), as is the brake wheel. The I-beams and channel structure (cradle) for the wood tanks was

Fig. 9-23. Snow plow pilot: detailing GP50.

Fig. 9-24. *Scratchbuilt superdetailed vinegar tank car. Model work by Carl Caiati.*

fashioned from Northeastern wood shapes glued with plastic cement. Trucks are Central Valley Bettendorfs. A Cal-Scale Westinghouse brake system was added for underbody detailing. Tanks were fashioned by cutting to size 1-inch-thick dowels that were then sheathed with 1/32-inch-wide Northeastern scribed sheathing.

The finished model was brush painted with Floquil engine black (frame) and Floquil Silver (tanks).

The tank car was hand-lettered with India ink and a 00 Rapidograph pen prior to an overall protection coating of clear flat enamel, which was also applied by brush. The model is shown here before weathering—as it would look coming out of the shop.

How far one can go in superdetailing depends on the ingenuity of the builder coupled with the availability of specialty additive castings and parts.

Chapter 10

Painting, Decaling, and Weathering

The final finishing touches in model railroading (as in virtually all scale modeling) involve painting and decorating.

Except for the pre-colored plastic kits available (structure and rolling stock), almost all models constructed are in need of finish painting (Fig. 10-1). Model railroad decorative work usually entails the addition or inclusion of decals—the final step with most freight cars, passenger cars, locomotives (road names, advertising) and some commercial structures (billboards, logos, company names).

Final finishing in model railroading goes one step further, encompassing a process called "weathering." Because all the integral modeling connected with railroading emulates outdoor situations and objects (all things outdoors are subjected to nature's elements), it is important that models are weathered either superficially or radically in order to exhibit added authenticity (Fig. 10-2).

With weathering, buildings, locomotives, rolling stock, vehicles, machinery, etc. are made to appear dirty, dingy, dusty, old, or beat up as if affected by the ravages of time and nature. This can be simulated on models with paint and color administered with brush, swab, or airbrush. This chapter deals with all the aforementioned aspects of final finishing, stressing authenticity and realism.

PAINTING

Paints

There are a number of manufactured paint mediums adaptable for railroad model painting and the modeler can take his pick from them. One paint medium in particular, however, stands high above the rest and was specifically formulated for model railroad use: Floquil. Floquil is a lacquer-type paint available in standard colors, and also in authentic railroad colors common to all the railroad lines in the United States. Floquil dries to a flat finish (another plus) and can be obtained in 1- or 2-ounce quantities (bottles). Some colors come also in spray cans, but these are not highly recommended because spray can painting it not exacting enough for finely scaled R.R. miniatures. Nor is the spray can very controllable.

Floquil is thinned with its own specific solvent called Dio-Sol. In cases where a slow drying time or better paint flowout is desired, a retarding agent is available that, when added to the paint, will slow down the drying time. Slow drying time can be very beneficial for airbrushing and large area painting. For painting on plastic, a barrier coat solution is offered that serves as a sealer and protects the plastic from Floquil lacquer that tends to etch unprotected plastic surfaces.

Floquil Poly S is another good paint for railroad application. Poly S needs no special solvent and is water soluble. Poly S colors are excellent for wood, plaster, and cardboard, but are not well suited to metal.

Painting Wood

Though Floquil is a universal medium equally suited for painting over wood or metal, the procedures differ in some respects. Metal surfaces take paint better and more uniformly when applied with the aid of an airbrush, while handbrushing is more ideally suited to wood. Wood can be airbrushed, but airbrushed lacquer tends to settle on the wood's surface rather than soak into it as when applied with a brush. Worked into the surface, the lacquer covering is more resilient and better looking (Fig. 10-3).

The best brushes to use for handpainting railroad models are the round red sables. The necessary brush sizes are the Nos. 1 and 2 for overall painting, and the 0 for fine detail work.

Don't scrimp when buying brushes; buy the best brushes possible because they will paint better and last longer. The better brushes are the ones marketed by Winsor Newton, Robert Simmons, and Grumbacher, and are more easily obtainable through the better art stores than hobby shops.

Prior to final color painting, Floquil recommends priming. For wood I prefer an alternate method: two coats of white shellac to seal the wood and prepare it for paint. Allow a day for drying time, then sand with 600 grit sandpaper. Shellac, followed by sanding, smooths the wood face and eliminates grainy or "fuzzy" surfaces which are natural characteristics of basswood and other woods.

Fig. 10-1. A craftsman wood kit simply painted.

Fig. 10-2. A lesser plastic kit of the same type pickle car. Note how painting and weathering can give a craftsmanlike appearance similar to car in Fig. 10-1.

Fig. 10-3. A scratchbuilt reefer by Carl Caiati. Model was brushpainted with Floquil lacquers and decorated with Walthers decals.

These woods should be treated in order to achieve fine, flawless paint coats.

Painting Metal

The painting of metal is an altogether different ball game. Model railroad metals or metal surfaces to be painted are of zamac (zinc aluminum casting), steel, aluminum or brass. These can all be brush painted, but for best results spray with an airbrush. Brush painting leaves streaks, while the airbrush will spray on an even, uniform, realistic-looking coat (Fig. 10-4).

The Airbrush. The airbrush has carved its niche in the art and hobby field. It is basically a scaled-down version of a spray gun, miniaturized in order to execute fine detail work.

There are two types of airbrushes marketed that are suited to model painting: the single action and the double action. They both contain movable needles that meter out the fluid or paint supply as the point of the needle is advanced or withdrawn through the air-fluid nozzle—which is the frontal portion and business end of the airbrush (Fig. 10-5).

In the single-action airbrush, the needle adjustment to govern spray width is set by turning a knob at the handle end of the airbrush. Clockwise sets the needle into the air nozzle, counterclockwise moves it out of the air nozzle. The further the needle is placed into the nozzle, the finer the spray pattern emitted. A good airbrush with a fine needle will allow you to do fine critical work and practically draw lines.

The double-action airbrush works on the same principle, except that it has built into it a spring-loaded, dual-action button that controls spray width and liquid metering by means of a common fingertip control button at the top of the airbrush barrel. The button has an on-off, up-and-down action coupled with a back-and-forth spray width control action. Press down on the button and air begins to flow. The air pressure should be set at the air supply source (usually a compressor) at about 25 pounds. As the button is pulled back (at the same time as it is depressed) the needle is withdrawn

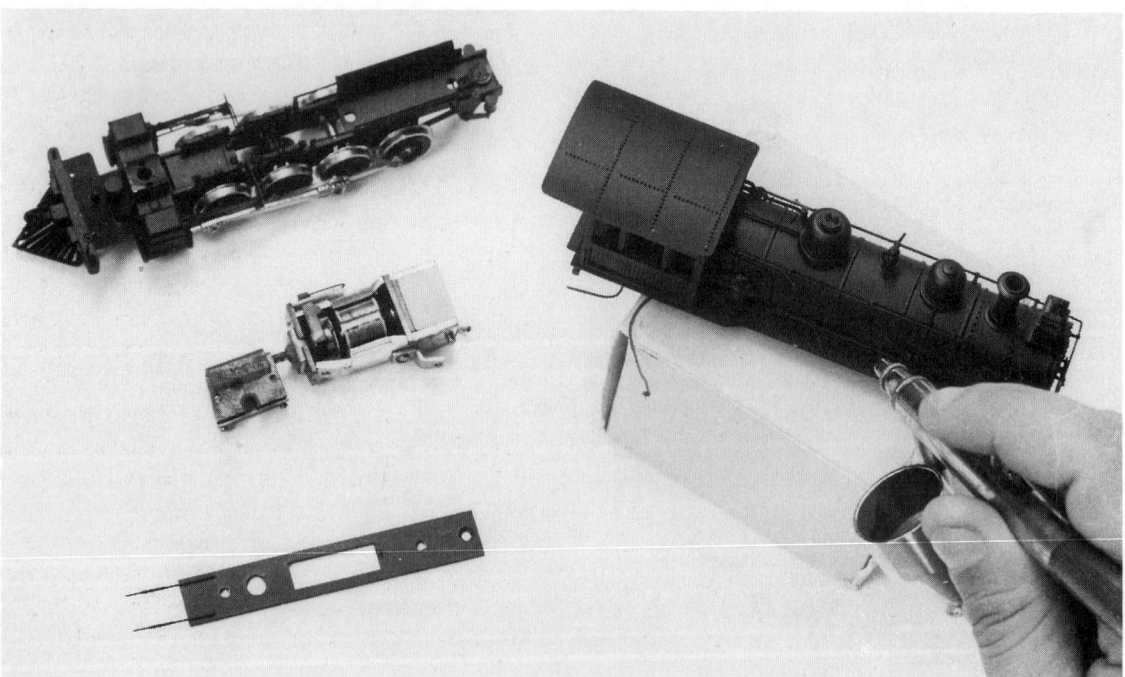

Fig. 10-4. Airbrushing is the accepted method for locos and metal rolling stock. Prior to painting, engines should be taken apart so that working parts and mechanisms are not oversprayed.

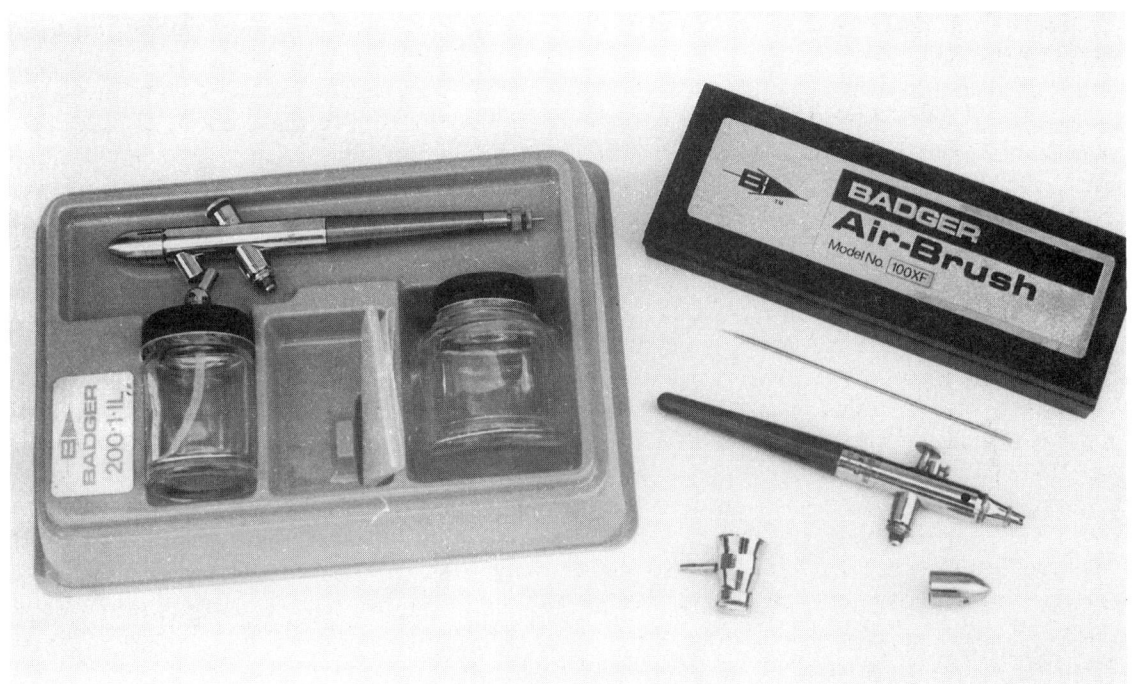

Fig. 10-5. The airbrush, a necessary painting tool. Shown are the Badger 200 (single action) and Badger 100 XF (double action).

from the nozzle opening and paint begins to flow through the orifice. The further back the button is slid, the more paint flows; at the same time the spray cone widens.

You can judge for yourself how much more versatile the double-action airbrush can be. Whether a single- or double-action model is chosen, keep in mind that you can get equally good results with both. The single action is cheaper, although as effective, in the long run. The flexibility of the double action makes it desirable, especially for more experienced modelmakers who "fine detail."

Two airbrushes I would enthusiastically recommend are the Badger 200 (single action) and the Badger 150 (dual action). They are about the finest, most trouble-free available for model painting and may be obtained at virtually all hobby and art shops.

When spraying large metal pieces (engines, passenger and freight cars), choose a wide spray setting for smooth and even coverage. Use heavy side-to-side strokes overlapping by a half stroke each consecutive stroke. For small detail work or fittings, spray with a finer spray width.

Prior to painting, metal must be properly prepared or prepped to insure good bonding between the paint and metal surface. Zamac should be sanded with 600 grit paper or etched in a bath of acetic acid (available at photo shops). After washing in water to remove excess acid, the zamac is airbrush-primed with Floquil grey primer. Brass also should be etched or "prickled" prior to painting. Floquil makes a special conditioner bath for this, or you can revert to the old standby acetic acid. Again, wash off, then coat with Floquil primer. Steel is rarely encountered, but if it must be painted, it should be sanded with 350 grit paper and then Floquil primed. Aluminum needs a special primer after sanding. Use two coats of zinc chromate primer, then paint the aluminum.

Painting Plastic. Plastic can be painted in much the same manner as metal with these following minor revisions: instead of primer, use the Floquil barrier coat (sprayed on) before you begin to paint. Floquil lacquers promote an etching action on some plastics, particularly if the paint is heavy in solvent content. The barrier coat will inhibit the plastic etching action of Floquil.

DECALING

After painting comes decaling, the decorative aspect of final model finishing (Fig. 10-6). Almost everyone has used decals at some time or other in their lives, so the application of decals should be no secret, as shown on the following pages. I would, however, like to pass on the following tips that will serve to make the finished, decorated scale model appear realistic and authentic.

- Cut as close to the lettering or logo as possible to minimize excess decal film area (Fig. 10-7).
- Apply decals over as smooth a surface as

possible in order to realize maximum adhesion.

- Don't oversaturate decals with water; just enough to allow the film to slip off the backing (Fig. 10-8).
- Don't handle decal film excessively with your fingers. Use tweezers whenever possible (Fig. 10-9).
- After placement, swab the decals with cotton or Q-tip to work out excess water and air bubbles (Fig. 10-10).
- Apply Walthers Solvaset to allow the decal to snuggle down tight against surface and to drape over surface texture such as rivets, fittings, scribed wood, etc. With scribed wood, if the decal bridges across the lines, allow the

Fig. 10-6. Decals of all types are available as are design and prototype lettering diagrams. Champion and Walthers are two of the leading decal producers.

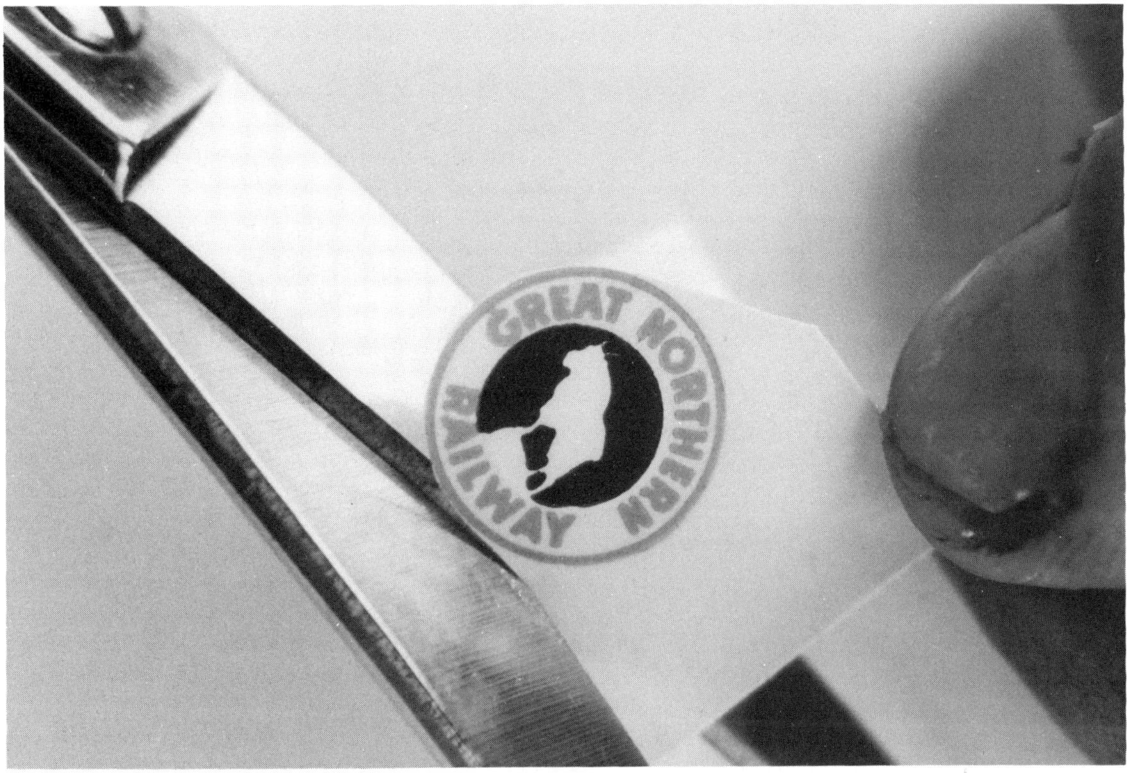

Fig. 10-7. Cut decal closely to minimize extraneous decal film.

Fig. 10-8. Immerse decal until softening and parting takes place.

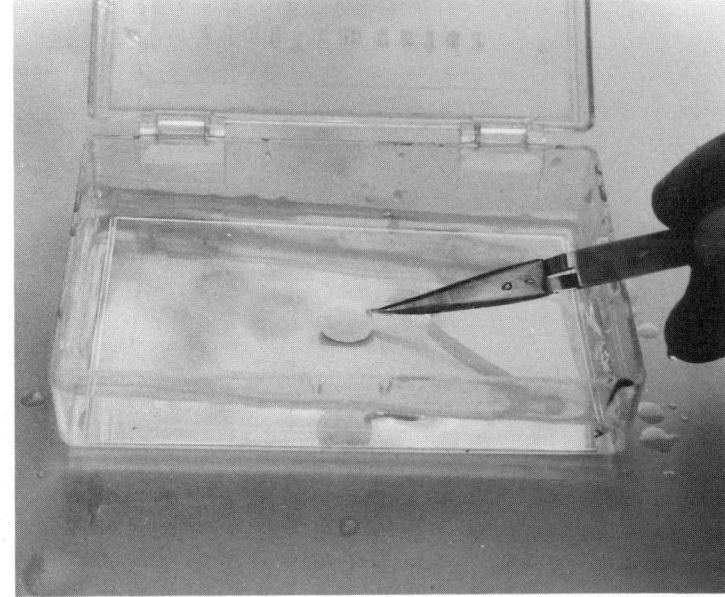

Fig. 10-9. Apply decal delicately with a tweezer.

decal to fully dry, then run a No. 11 X-acto blade between scribing, cutting the decal while affixed in its respective place. Then add a drop of Solvaset on the decal again and it should then conform to the scribed wood as desired (Figs. 10-11 and 10-12).

• After decals have fully dried, spray the model with Walthers DDV or Floquil matte

spray coating. This will kill the decal's shine and give the model an overall dull, realistic finish (Fig. 10-13).

WEATHERING

Hand or spray weathering are the acknowledged aging procedures in railroad modeling. Weathering is an easy technique to learn. Prior to tackling

Fig. 10-10. Dab away excess water with a cotton cloth.

Fig. 10-11. Abolish air bubbles by piercing with knifepoint or pin.

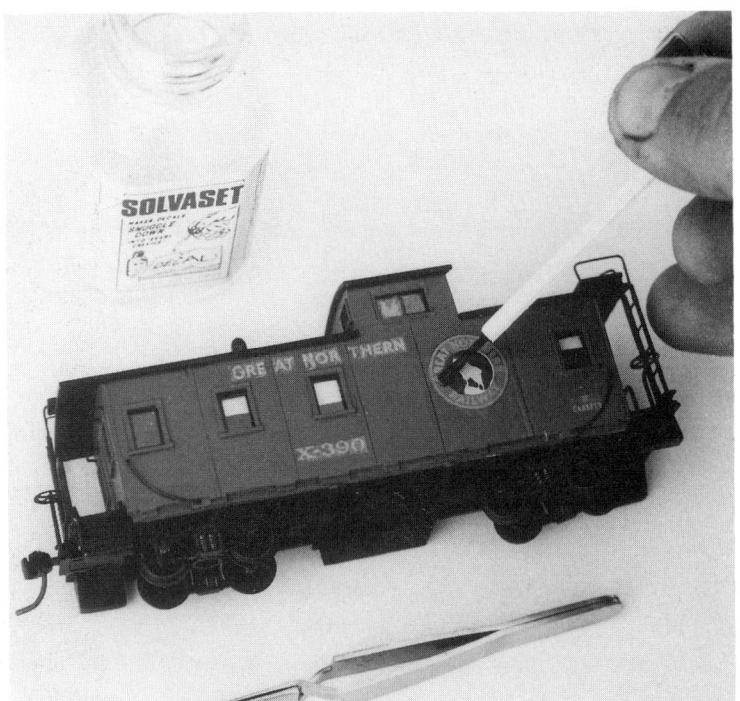

Fig. 10-12. Apply Solvaset to make decals snuggle down.

Fig. 10-13. Proper and well-placed decaling with no trace of a "decal" look.

weathering and aging, study prototype situations to familiarize yourself as to what transpires when structures or rolling stock get old or are exposed to the elements (Figs. 10-14 through 10-16).

Oil Stains

My favorite is the oil stain technique, using oil paints with turpentine as a thinning agent. You can employ thin washes for color smudge buildups, or use the drybrush method. Raw umber and black make excellent washes and may be applied with a dry or wet brush. Achieve the thinning ratio through individual practice and experimentation. Oil stains dry slowly so that they can be rubbed down to minimize intensity if overapplied. Q-tips also are excellent for working weathering stains onto painted metal surfaces or wood.

To get a stronger effect, use drybrushing. For overall dirt and dust highlighting, you can use airbrushing, which gives dust haze effects over large areas. Zinc white in a very thinned-out state works well for this.

Floquil makes an excellent weathering kit containing dust, rust, grime, etc. The dust coloring is best applied with an airbrush; rust and grime best

Fig. 10-14. Combined weathering techniques for engines begin with airbrushing to simulate dirt and dust.

Fig. 10-15. Stronger detailing and effects are added with brushing.

administered by the drybrush method.

A number of weathered pieces are illustrated within this chapter and in the color section of this book. Note how various weathering applications add to the authenticity of the finished model (Figs. 19-17 through 10-23).

The photo on page 127 shows a typical old-time Pabst billboard unit seen on national railroads frequently in the 1920s and 1930s. Billboard reefers were a prime advertising vehicle and were kept, if not in new condition, at least legible. The model shown here is not overly weathered and certainly

Fig. 10-16. Finished, weathered Max Gray three-truck Shay.

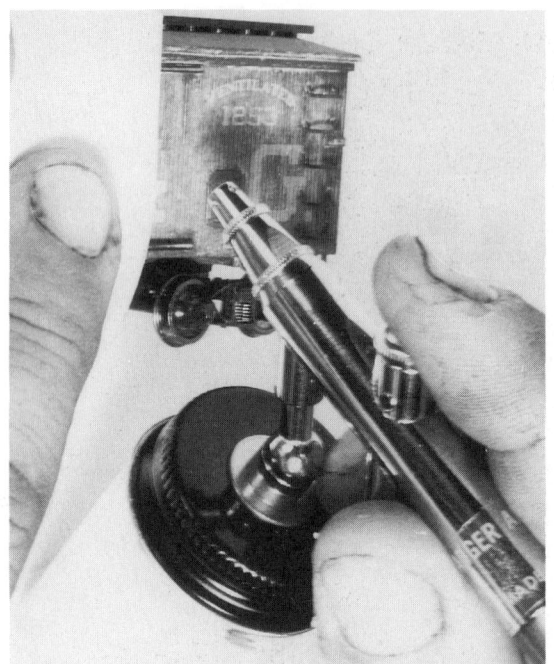

Fig. 10-17. Sheathing is airbrushed with Floquil "dust." Straight edge of card is used to mask each consecutively weathered plank to obtain contrasting degrees of weathering as on actual weathered wood.

not aged because the model pike it runs on is a 1930 period pike.

Here's how this piece was enhanced with realistic and valid weathering: The lettering was streaked and dusted (note the "b" and "t" in the word "Pabst") with a OO Winsor Newton red sable brush and while oil coloring. The streaking was drybrushed and blended in. The planks on the sides of the car were alternately streaked with shellac (for a new replaced board look) and other planks were streaked with grey oil stain washes to simulate time discoloration, soot, grime, etc. Hinges and metal pieces on the door were smudged with powdered graphite to imitate the worn metal look on freight car doors that experience frequent usage. Thinned-out sepia stain was administered at one end with a stain-laden brush and allowed to flow along the cracks. Note the separation between planks due to the stain introduced between them. Floquil dust was applied to the roof with an airbrush. Floquil rust was delicately and sporadically applied by brush tip at the proper locations on all metalwork, such as door hinges, trucks, ladders, metal fittings, and roof hatches. Black paint coating on hatches

Fig. 10-18. Note effect obtained with this method.

Fig. 10-19. For comparison; right section from door is weathered.

Fig. 10-20. Weathering the wood flooring on this pulpwood car gives it a used look.

Fig. 10-21. The airbrush is also very effective for large area weathering, as on structures.

Fig. 10-22. The oil wash method applied to a shingled roof.

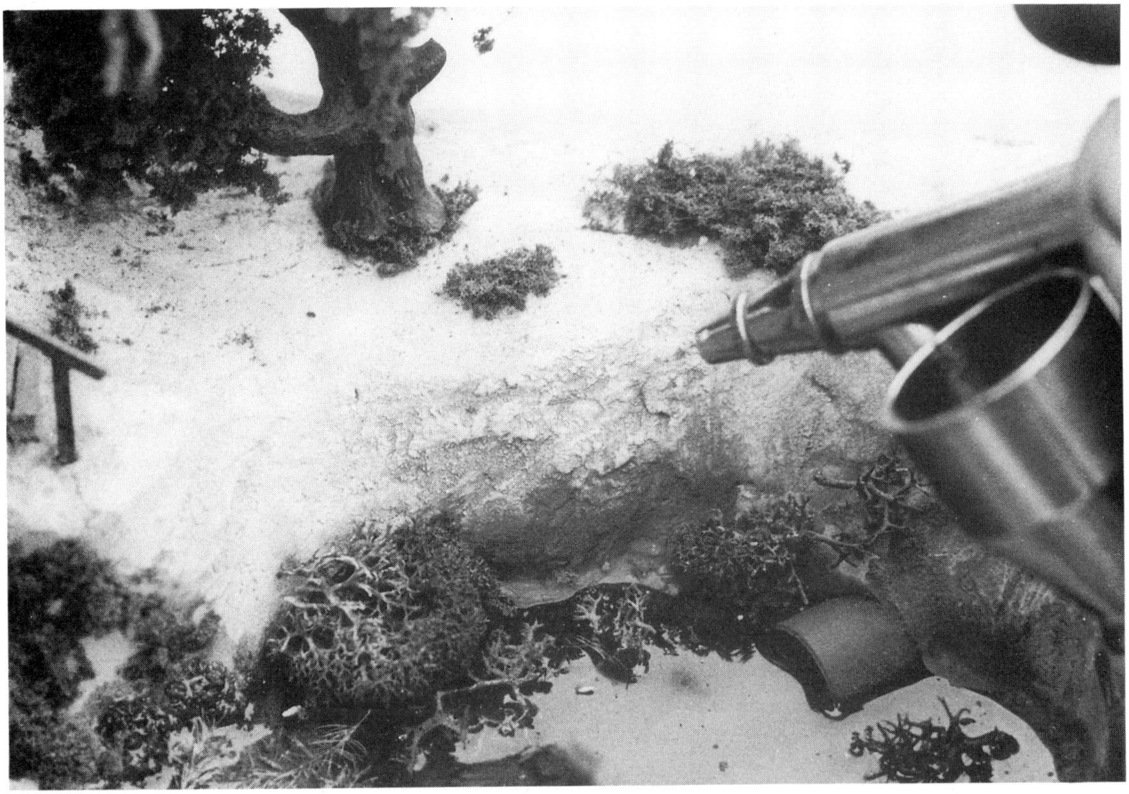

Fig. 10-23. Airbrushing is also effective in shading and tinting scenic details.

Fig. 10-24. A pair of AHM E8's, Seaboard R.R. Painted and detailed by Lou Kozla.

Fig. 10-25. Alco FA. Original paint scheme.

was scratched with a No. 11 X-acto blade (on the corners, bolts, etc.) to simulate wear.

Figures 10-24 and 10-25 are prime examples of well-painted, well-decaled, properly executed model facsimiles of prototypes by Lou Kozla. Lou models ACL and Seaboard stock. Three outstanding examples are presented here.

Figure 10-24 (top) shows an AHM E8 that Lou decorated in the original Seaboard Airline trim. Clean masking and fine, exacting decal work went into this one. Lou used Poly S colors applied with an airbrush. The overall base color coat was first administered. Then the base paint was masked off with 3M fine line tape and the second color was air-

brushed over the first. Micro Scale decals provided the finishing touches. Liberal applications of Solvaset allowed the decals to snuggle down and conform to the diesel's body lines and detail etching. An overall coat of DDV was applied (matte varnish) to kill the decal shine and hide the edges. The diesel unit underneath is another E-8 but with the last SAL color scheme prior to the Seaboard Airline and Atlantic Coast Line Merger.

Another beauty from Lou's roster is the Alco FA in Fig. 10-25. Here again we witness Lou's attention to detail and clean workmanship. This Alco sports the original delivery color scheme and decorative styling.

Chapter 11

Couplers and Coupling

L ast but by no means least, a bit of space should be delegated to couplers and coupling, since the mechanisms and the functions they perform are so crucial to prototype railroad (as well as model) operation.

Couplers should be as attractive and as true to prototype in appearance as they are functional. Unfortunately, in this hobby functionality supercedes appearance, so the final results provide good operating couplers but with slight deviations off the prototype norm (which we can easily live with).

In the early model railroading days we had to live with the cast plastic or zamac dummy couplers (Fig. 11-1). These were prototypical in size and appearance but static; the knuckles were inoperative. Trains and cars were coupled by hand slipping one coupler into another as the individual cars were laid on the track. Later on, some companies like Kemtron added to their dummy coupler line working couplers (Fig. 11-2) which could be opened by means of a rod activated by hand or a ramp set into the track. Then, a little over 20 years ago, the NMRA approved and sanctioned a working coupler, which became known as the NMRA coupler. It was accepted as the industry standard and still enjoys popularity today (Fig. 11-3).

The big problem with the NMRA coupler (though it is operationally very functional and trustworthy) is that it is obtuse designwise and many modelers are opposed to its unprototypical appearance. The more recently designed and best types by Rail Line offer magnetic uncoupling, a good plus feature.

Fig. 11-2. An early Kemtron type working coupler.

Next came the Kadee coupler. The Kadee also is a superb operative coupler that works magnetically—and flawlessly. The best feature with the Kadee coupler is its appearance, which emulates prototype detailing. The only shortcoming of the Kadee Magnematic coupler is that it is slightly oversize (out of scale). This is, however, a most negligible factor and has not stopped the Kadee from gaining a favored position as the best all-around coupler.

The newer Kadee delayed action coupling system allows engines over one uncoupling mechanism (an electro or permanent magnet) to manipulate cars at other points on any track beyond the magnet.

Kadee couplers may be obtained at any model railroad supplier, backed up with a complete system of uncoupling magnets, detailed instructions, height gauges, and some with their own draft gear (Fig. 11-4 shows the No. 7 underset coupler package). The Kadee coupler line is so complete and variable that there is a Kadee for every known sit-

Fig. 11-1. Some vintage cast couplers.

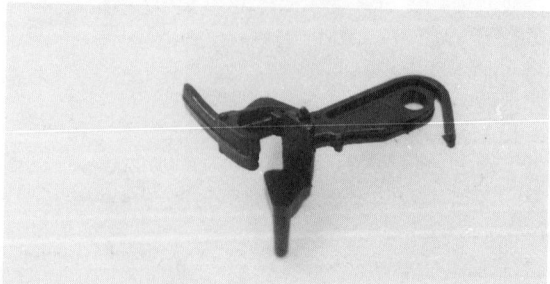

Fig. 11-3. The standard but not overly attractive NMRA coupler.

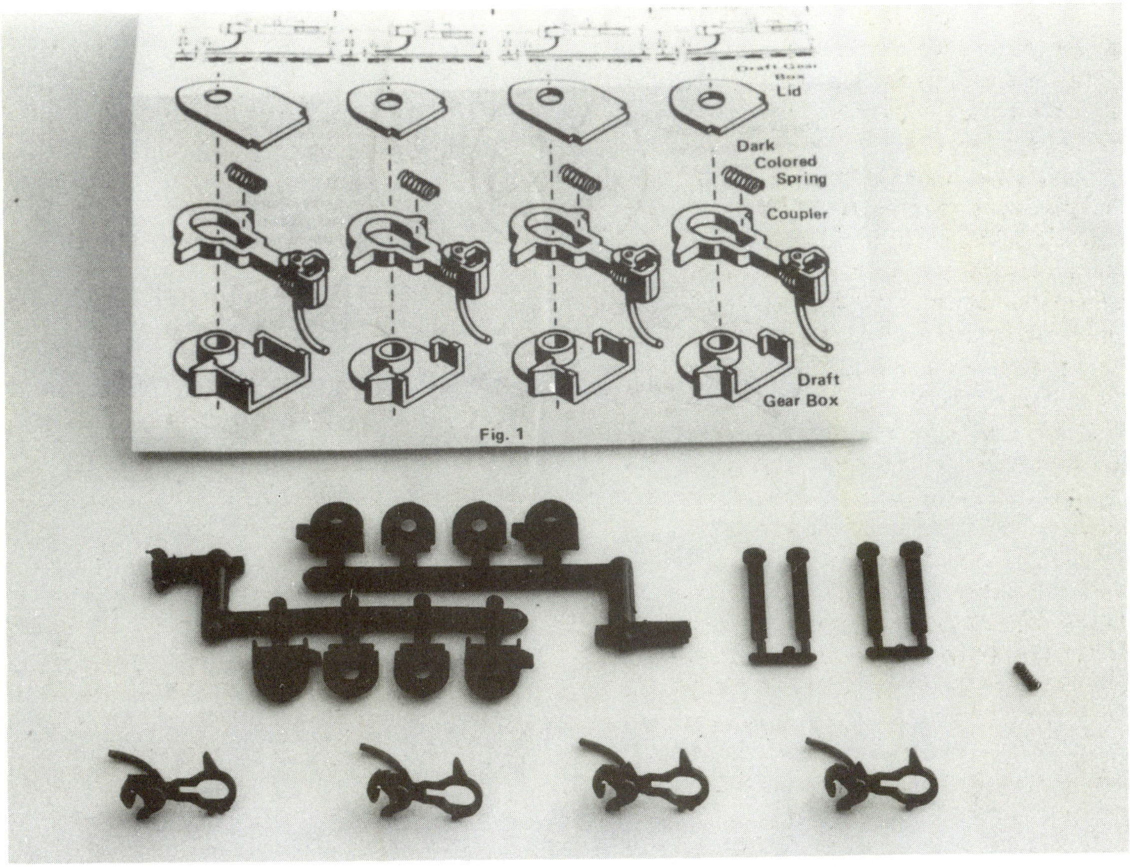

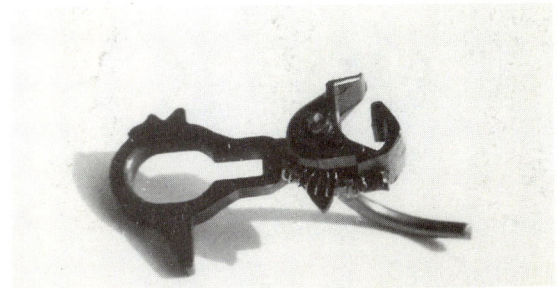

Fig. 11-4. The Kadee "C" shank couplers as packaged. Simple assembly puts them in quick working order.

uation. In HO scale there are about eight different types and configurations.

Shank style "C" was basically formulated for locomotive pilot and other tight or out-of-the-ordinary situations. It comes in four types:

- No. 6—A long coupler and large draft gear for long pilots and similar gear end situations.
- No. 7—An underset coupler for low platforms and tight clearances with a smaller draft gear.
- No. 8—Another short draft type but without underset.
- No. 16—Features longest shank and shortest draft box, primarily used for European equipment.

Type "C" shank couplers may be mounted with 2-56 tap into the pilot beam and a 2-56 screw. If coupler and assembled draft gear will not slip through pilot beam openings (as in most cases) the coupler and gear may be assembled directly on the pilot beam. Coupler assembly is simple and the in-

Fig. 11-5. Kadee No. 7 coupler with the "C" shank.

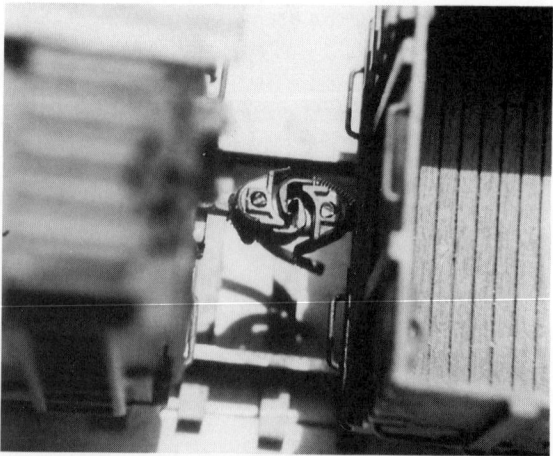

Fig. 11-6. The "C" shank coupler mounted on a car that has an end sill as opposed to full coupler pocket.

structions provided are explicit for all situations utilizing the "C" shank Kadee (Figs. 11-5 and 11-6).

Another Kadee type is the No. 5 coupler that features the style "B" shank and comes designed

Fig. 11-7. The Kadee "B" shank coupler complete with draft gear.

Fig. 11-8. The Kadee coupler in locked position.

for mounting in its own draft gear box. This type coupler is for use on cars where the draft gear boxes are not supplied or not cast into the body (Fig. 11-5). Couplers are attached by mounting the entire draft gear box with 2-56 screws or tiny wood screws. The No. 5 couplers are ideal for Atheam Train Miniature and roundhouse type cars (Fig. 11-8).

Another shank style "A" is also available that is similar to style "B" but with a back-and-forth spring buffing action.

For some situations (as in loco pilots) you might want to revert to scale detailed dummy units. Cal-Scale makes two excellent brass cast dummy couplers that are finely detailed. Kemtron has some fine brass coupler pockets as well, and also supplies hard-to-find old-style link and pin couplers. If you want to dress up and detail your coupling area, Cal-Scale makes some air hose castings that can be located right next to couplers and coupler pockets. Fancy coupler hosework for diesel loco application can be obtained from Detail Associates.

For the best information and coupler listings, consult the Walthers catalog—which features every type of coupler and related gear imaginable.

Sources

There was a time (unfortunately many years ago) when you could walk into a model railroad or hobby shop and find everything you needed from parts to tooling at your fingertips. Those were the days when hobbyshops were run by hobbyists themselves who took a sincere interest in plying their wares, with a backup of knowledgeable advice: Today, the hobbyshop is basically a commercial venture and—because it is no longer a very lucrative venture—today's hobby and train shops will only stock fast-moving, saleable items. Though the purist hobby shop owner has fallen by the wayside, we do have a proliferation of products, accessories, and scratchbuilding supplies and equipment far more sophisticated than the offerings available years ago, when the scratchbuilder had to rely on his craftsmanship and expertise. Granted, many of the materials and products specified in this book might not be readily available first hand, but they are obtainable if one knows how.

The two best approaches to obtaining your necessities is by special order from your local hobby shop or mail order: both take time and patience on the part of the buyer.

When using a hobby or model railroad shop as a source, know the part you want, the part or kit number, and the manufacturer. If, for instance, the shop utilizes Walthers as a distributor, you are in luck because Walthers is the best-stocked distributor of model railroad parts servicing the country. Their ability to obtain parts is fast and reliable—second to none. Unfortunately, because Walthers is primarily a distributor they do not ship or sell to the average consumer. You can, however, obtain a Walthers catalog, which will become your bible—offering a wealth of knowledge and an unlimited stock of any part kit or tool you require or desire. The huge Walthers catalog can be obtained by sending $12.95 to:

Walthers
5601 West Florist Avenue
Milwaukee, WI 53218

The catalog is worth every penny and is an advised investment for HO rail buffs.

Bowser Manufacturing Co. is also considered an excellent source for kits, materials, tools, etc., and they do retail to the consumer directly by mail, offering speedy and efficient service. They provide a massive catalog that can be obtained by sending $6.95 to:

Bowser Manufacturing Co.
21 Howard Street
Montoursville, PA 17754

This catalog is another must for the railroad modelers bookcase.

Following is a categorized listing of material and general sources, most of which are featured in this book. They can also be considered a mail-order source since virtually all will service you directly if you have no alternate sources. Check frequently the pages of *Model Railroader* and *Railroad Model Craftsman*. They always list and feature mail-order suppliers and manufacturers in addition to new parts and products listings.

Airbrushes

Badger Airbrush Co.
9128 West Belmont Avenue
Franklin Park, IL

Bridge Trestle Kits

Campbell Scale Models
P. O. Box 121
Tustin, CA 92680

Crummy Products
5655 Beechnut
Houston, TX 77096

Craftsman Car Kits-Rolling Stock

Central Valley
13000 Saticoy Street
No. Hollywood, CA 91605

Diamond Scale Construction
Box 691
Oakridge, OR 97643

Kadee
720 Grape Street
Medford, OR 97501
(logging cars)

Model Die Casting
3811 West Rosecrans Avenue
Hawthorne, CA 90250

Northeastern Scale Models, Inc.
Box 425
Methuen, MA 01844
(quality basswood)

Precision Scale Co., Inc. (brass kits, etc.)
1120 A Gum Avenue
Woodland, CA 95695

Custom Backdrops (Scenics)

Detail Associates
Box 197
Santa Maria, CA 93456

Wm. K. Walthers, Inc.
5601 West Florist Avenue
Milwaukee, WI 53218

Decals (Rolling Stock, Engines, etc.)

Champ Decals
Box 1178 R
Minot, ND 58701

Clover House
Box 62
Sebastopol, CA 95472
(dry transfer lettering)

Custom Decals (made to order)
Minirail
Box 293
Berwyn, IL 60402

D M Custom Decals
2127 South 11th Street
Manitowoc, WI 54220

Krasel Industries, Inc.
1821 East Newport Circle
Santa Ana, CA 92705

Miller Advertising
1627 Lilac Drive
Manitowoc, WI 54220
(catalog with diagrams $5.00)

Figures and Animals

Stevens International
Box 2908
Cherry Hill, NJ 08034

Weston Division of Campbell Scale Models
Box 121
Tustin, CA 92680

Woodland Scenics
Box 266
Shawnee Mission, KS 66201

Freight and Passenger Car Trucks

Hallmark Models, Inc.
4822 Bryan Street
Dallas, TX 75204

Model Die Casting
Box 926
Hawthorne, CA 90250

Houses-Industrial Structures

Chooch Enterprises, Inc.
2658 Honolulu Blvd.
Montrose, CA 91020

Columbia Valley Model
Box 2206
Bellingham, WA 98227

E. Suydam & Co.
Box 55
Duarte, CA 01010

Evergreen Hill Designs
Box 633
Los Molinos, CA 96055

Keystone Locomotive Works
159 Wheatley Avenue
Northumberland, PA 17857

Life Like Products, Inc.
Baltimore, MD 21211

Magnuson Models, Inc.
Box 199
Lake Villa, IL 60046

Muir Models, Inc.
2020 East South Susan
Santa Ana, CA 92704

Paint

(Wood stains, authentic R. R. colors weathering paint)

Floquil Poly S Color Corp.
Route 30 N
Amsterdam, NY 12010

Scratch Building Materials

(Brass—tubing, rod, channel, angle, sheet brass)

K & S Engineering
6917 West 59th Street
Chicago, IL

Milled Shapes, Inc.
1701 North 33rd Avenue
Melrose Park, IL 60160

Special Shapes, Co.
P. O. Box 487
Romeoville, IL

(Styrene)

Evergreen Scale Models, Inc.
2685-151st Place N. E.
Redmond, WA 98052

(Wood—structural milled shapes, stripwood, rolling stock roofs, flooring, ends, bolsters, sheathing, etc.)

Northeastern Scale Models, Inc.
Box 425
Methuen, MA 01844

Perfection Hardwoods (Bass, Walnut, Cherry, Mahog., Balsa)
P. O. Box 52 C
Hobart, IN 46342

Signals

Caboose Industries
1861 North Ridge Drive
Freeport, IL 61032
(switch stands)

Century Foundry & Metal Works
Box 177
North Hollywood, CA 91603

N. J. International, Inc.
77 West Nicholas Street
Hicksville, NY 11801

Tower Engineering
Box 32
Valley Stream, NY 11582
(switch signal lights)

Superdetailing Parts and Components
(Interior/exterior detailing)

Cal-Scale
Box 475
Pinedale, CA 93650

Precision Scale Co., Inc.
1120 - A Gum Avenue
Woodland, CA 95695

Track and Rail

Atlas Tool Co.
378 Florence Avenue
Hillside, NJ 07205
(sectional track and turnouts)

Gargraves Trackage Corp.
Box 255 A
North Rose, NY 14516

Lambert Associates
Box 4338
San Leandro, CA 94579
(rail in Code 100, Code 70)

M. L. R. Manufacturing
Box 1051
Carlsbad, CA 92008
(track and ballast laying tools)

Nickel Plate Products
301 Halsted Street
Chicago Heights, IL 60411
(Code 100 turnouts)

Tru-Scale
Box 8157
Prairie Village, KS 66208

Trees and Shubbery

Campbell
P. O. Box 121
Tustin, CA 92680
(pine tree kits)

Durango Press
Box 1836
Lynnwood, WA 98036
(instant weeds)